D0194856

CONSTITUTIONAL
AMENDMENTS
BEYOND THE BILL OF RIGHTS

Amendment XXVI
Lowering the Voting Age

Other Books of Related Interest

Opposing Viewpoints Series

Civil Liberties

Feminism

Race Relations

Work

Working Women

Current Controversies Series

Civil Liberties

Extremist Groups

Feminism

Human Rights

CONSTITUTIONAL
AMENDMENTS
BEYOND THE BILL OF RIGHTS

Amendment XXVI
Lowering the Voting Age

Sylvia Engdahl, Book Editor

GREENHAVEN PRESS
A part of Gale, Cengage Learning

Detroit • New York • San Francisco • New Haven, Conn • Waterville, Maine • London

GALE
CENGAGE Learning·

Christine Nasso, *Publisher*
Elizabeth Des Chenes, *Managing Editor*

© 2010 Greenhaven Press, a part of Gale, Cengage Learning.

Gale and Greenhaven Press are registered trademarks used herein under license.

For more information, contact:
Greenhaven Press
27500 Drake Rd.
Farmington Hills, MI 48331-3535
Or you can visit our Internet site at gale.cengage.com

For product information and technology assistance, contact us at

Gale Customer Support, 1-800-877-4253
For permission to use material from this text or product, submit all requests online at
www.cengage.com/permissions

Further permissions questions can be emailed to permissionrequest@cengage.com

Articles in Greenhaven Press anthologies are often edited for length to meet page requirements. In addition, original titles of these works are changed to clearly present the main thesis and to explicitly indicate the author's opinion. Every effort is made to ensure that Greenhaven Press accurately reflects the original intent of the authors. Every effort has been made to trace the owners of copyrighted material.

Cover photograph © Sandy Huffaker/Getty Images.

LIBRARY OF CONGRESS CATALOGING-IN-PUBLICATION DATA

Amendment XXVI : lowering the voting age / Sylvia Engdahl, book editor.
   p. cm. -- (Constitutional amendments: beyond the Bill of Rights)
   Includes bibliographical references and index.
   ISBN 978-0-7377-4453-8 (hardcover)
   1. United States. Constitution. 26th Amendment. 2. Voting age--Law and legislation--United States--History--20th century--Juvenile literature. I. Engdahl, Sylvia.
   KF4891.A467 2009
   342.73'072--dc22

                                          2009018934

Printed in the United States of America
1 2 3 4 5 6 7 13 12 11 10 09

Contents

Chapter 1: Historical Background on the Twenty-sixth Amendment

Chapter 2: Constitutional Implications of the New Law

Chapter 3: Amendment XXVI and Its Consequences

Chapter 4: The Youth Vote in Contemporary America

Appendices

Lowering the Voting Age

"Today's Constitution is a realistic document of freedom only because of several corrective amendments. Those amendments speak to a sense of decency and fairness."

Thurgood Marshall

While the U.S. Constitution forms the backbone of American democracy, the amendments make the Constitution a living, ever-evolving document. Interpretation and analysis of the Constitution inform lively debate in every branch of government, as well as among students, scholars, and all other citizens, and views on various articles of the Constitution have changed over the generations. Formally altering the Constitution, however, can happen only through the amendment process. The Greenhaven Press series The Bill of Rights examines the first ten amendments to the Constitution. Constitutional Amendments: Beyond the Bill of Rights continues the exploration, addressing key amendments ratified since 1791.

The process of amending the Constitution is painstaking. While other options are available, the method used for nearly every amendment begins with a congressional bill that must pass both the Senate and the House of Representatives by a two-thirds majority. Then the amendment must be ratified by three-quarters of the states. Many amendments have been proposed since the Bill of Rights was adopted in 1791, but only seventeen have been ratified.

It may be difficult to imagine a United States where women and African Americans are prohibited from voting, where the federal government allows one human being to enslave another, or where some citizens are denied equal protection under the law. While many of our most fundamental liberties are protected by the Bill of Rights, the amendments that followed have significantly broadened and enhanced the rights of American citizens. Such rights may be taken for granted today, but when the amendments were ratified, many were considered groundbreaking and proved to be explosively controversial.

Each volume in Constitutional Amendments provides an in-depth exploration of an amendment and its impact through primary and secondary sources, both historical and contemporary. Primary sources include landmark Supreme Court rulings, speeches by prominent experts, and newspaper editorials. Secondary sources include historical analyses, law journal articles, book excerpts, and magazine articles. Each volume first presents the historical background of the amendment, creating a colorful picture of the circumstances surrounding the amendment's passage: the campaigns to sway public opinion, the congressional debates, and the struggle for ratification. Next, each volume examines the ways the court system has been used to test the validity of the amendment and addresses the ramifications of the amendment's passage. The final chapter of each volume presents viewpoints that explore current controversies and debates relating to ways in which the amendment affects our everyday lives.

Numerous features are included in each Constitutional Amendments volume:

- An originally written introduction presents a concise yet thorough overview of the amendment.

- A time line provides historical context by describing key events, organizations, and people relating to the ratification of the amendment, subsequent court cases, and the impact of the amendment.

- An annotated table of contents offers an at-a-glance summary of each primary and secondary source essay included in the volume.

- The complete text of the amendment, followed by a "plain English" explanation, brings the amendment into clear focus for students and other readers.

- Graphs, charts, tables, and maps enhance the text.

- A list of all twenty-seven Constitutional Amendments offers quick reference.

- An annotated list of court cases relevant to the amendment broadens the reader's understanding of the judiciary's role in interpreting the Constitution.

- A bibliography of books, periodicals, and Web sites aids readers in further research.

- A detailed subject index allows readers to quickly find the information they need.

With the aid of this series, students and other researchers will become better informed of their rights and responsibilities as American citizens. Constitutional Amendments: Beyond the Bill of Rights examines the roots of American democracy, bringing to life the ways the Constitution has evolved and how it has impacted this nation's history.

Amendment Text and Explanation

The Twenty-sixth Amendment to the United States Constitution

Passed by Congress March 23, 1971. Ratified July 1, 1971.

Note: Section 2 of the Fourteenth Amendment (which specifies age twenty-one as the minimum for full citizenship rights) was modified by section 1 of the Twenty-sixth Amendment.

Section 1. The right of citizens of the United States, who are eighteen years of age or older, to vote shall not be denied or abridged by the United States or by any State on account of age.

Section 2. The Congress shall have power to enforce this article by appropriate legislation

Explanation

No citizen of the United States who is eighteen or older can be denied the right to vote in a federal or state election because of age.

Introduction

To today's teens, the prospect of being able to vote at age eighteen is taken for granted. But this is a relatively new development. Throughout most of the nation's history, citizens could not vote until the age of twenty-one, and except in a few states, no one alive today who was born before 1949 voted in a national election when younger than that. Twenty-one, rather than eighteen, was the age at which people were considered legal adults for most purposes, though now it has become a milestone only in connection with drinking alcohol.

Twenty-one was adopted as the age of majority in colonial America merely because that was the tradition in England, which some say originated as the age when men in medieval times were considered ready for knighthood. Yet in early America—and in England, too—young people functioned as adults much earlier than they do today. They married at a younger age, and men were expected to serve in the army beginning at age sixteen. There was no distinct class of teenagers; people went directly from childhood to the responsibilities of adulthood. It may therefore seem strange that older teens were not allowed to vote. However, at that time voting was not viewed as the right of all citizens. In the beginning, only men who owned property could vote. The idea of extending the franchise to everyone was simply unheard of.

Gradually, this changed. First, the right to vote was given to all white men except felons, whether or not they owned property (in a few states, only those who paid taxes could vote). After the Civil War, it was given to black men by the Fifteenth Amendment to the Constitution. Women did not gain the right to vote in most states until adoption of the Nineteenth Amendment in 1920, although in some states they received it a few years earlier. It was not granted to Native Americans, with the exception of those who served in World War I, until 1924.

Apart from constitutional amendments, voter qualifications are set by the states—the original Constitution does not
give the federal government any power to do so. Thus, although the voting age remained at twenty-one in all the states,
there were local exceptions—for example, in colonial times
there were some military elections in which all members of
the army participated, and for a brief period during formation
of the new nation, New Jersey's constitution permitted
property-owning blacks and women to vote. But the idea of
expanding the franchise was not welcomed by political leaders. One of the nation's principal founders, John Adams, wrote
to a member of the Massachusetts legislature:

> Depend on it, sir, it is dangerous to open so fruitful a source
> of controversy and altercation as would be opened by at-
> tempting to alter the qualifications of voters; there will be
> no end of it. New claims will arise: women will demand a
> vote; lads from twelve to twenty-one will think their rights
> not enough attended to; and every man who has not a far-
> thing [a coin worth a quarter-cent] will demand an equal
> voice with any other in all acts of state.

The first official attempt to lower the voting age occurred
in Missouri, in 1820, when a measure to do so lost by a vote
of two to one at a state convention. The next year, at a New
York constitutional convention, the idea that a man old
enough to fight was old enough to vote was debated for the
first time. Later, in 1867, several measures to grant the vote to
men between eighteen and twenty-one were proposed and defeated. There were various local proposals to let eighteen- to
twenty-year-olds vote after that, but not until the 1920s, after
the First World War in which many young Americans served,
did it become a topic of national interest. At that time, as
educational consultant Wendell W. Cultice has written in
Youth's Battle for the Ballot:

> It appeared to more than a few politicians and advocates of
> deferred suffrage, however, that it might be a sound move to

keep all youth out of politics. They believed that an attempt should be made to show that classroom work and politics could not mix. The public was warned that once in politics, youth would be at the mercy of demagogues, charlatans, and emotionally irresponsible people. The tangible and intangible consequences of political error or defeat would be, the guardians of youth contended, too many for immature minds to weigh them fully.

These views were prominent in the later debate after which young people did gain the right to vote, and they remain so today among opponents of recent proposals to lower the voting age still further. They reflect a fundamental change in the basis of citizen political awareness that has occurred since the United States was founded. In early America, it was assumed that most people had little or no knowledge of political issues beyond the desire for freedom. The U.S. government was based on representation rather than direct government by vote, not only for the practical reason that communication and travel between different regions was slow, but because it was believed that only men of exceptional experience and wisdom were qualified to make laws. If someone of that era had been asked why young people—or women, for that matter—should not have a voice in choosing representatives, one of the reasons given would probably have been that they lacked opportunity to become acquainted with men fit to represent them. Senators at that time were chosen by state legislatures, which were composed of men known locally. The president of the United States was elected not by the public, but indirectly by electors chosen for that purpose (which is still true today, though it has become a fiction retained merely to balance power among the states, and most voters do not even know the names of the electors pledged to vote for the presidential candidate they favor). The average voter's job was to pick local representatives worthy of trust.

Since the mid-nineteenth century, however, and with increasing speed in the twentieth and twenty-first, universal education and mass media have made knowledge of political issues available to everyone. The media have enabled candidates for office to make themselves known to the public at large. On one hand, this has meant that young people are better informed about issues than they were when the nation was founded. But on the other hand, it has indeed made them susceptible to persuasion by media celebrities. Both opponents of the youth vote and politicians hoping to take advantage of it have felt that inexperience might sway teens to make choices based more on emotion than on reason.

Advocates of the eighteen-year-old vote believed that this danger was outweighed by the argument that men old enough to fight should have the vote, which became common at the time of World War II. This idea was widely accepted, although some commentators pointed out that the implied comparison between fighting ability and voting ability was not valid—for example, congressman Emanuel Celler, who said, "To my mind, the draft age and the voting age are as different as chalk is from cheese. The thing called for in a soldier is uncritical obedience, and that is not what you want in a voter."

The real force of the argument was not derived from any connection between having the maturity to fight and being mature enough to vote wisely—after all, sixteen-year-olds and even younger boys had been serving as soldiers since the nation's beginning, and long before. Rather, it was based on a growing belief that since the right to vote was no longer restricted by anything but age, it was unfair for teens to be drafted into military service by government officials they had no voice in electing. However, there was strong public support for America's involvement in World War II and most young men felt it was their duty to fight. Many were eager to; some feared the war would be over before they got a chance to see action. So although lowering the voting age was often proposed, not enough people favored it for anything to be done.

By the time of the Vietnam War, the situation was different. The Vietnam War was an unpopular one, especially among young people, and large numbers of them resented being drafted to fight in it. The unfairness of their being unable to vote for the nation's leaders became a major issue among adults as well as teens, in part because nearly half the American soldiers who died in Vietnam were under twenty-one. A few states had already lowered the voting age, but in a number of others, measures to do so had been defeated. Congress decided that it was time to act. Yet the Constitution did not authorize Congress to set a national voting age—or did it? Many members of Congress believed that the Fourteenth Amendment, which provides for federal enforcement of the equal protection clause, gave it that power. Therefore, a provision lowering the voting age to eighteen was added to the Voting Rights Act of 1970, which was mainly concerned with banning the discriminatory voting practices of some states that had resulted in the disenfranchisement of blacks.

Some who favored lowering the voting age, including President Richard Nixon, had warned that the Voting Rights Act would be struck down by the courts and that a new constitutional amendment would be required, as it had been to extend the vote to women. Before long, Oregon, one of the states in which a previous attempt to allow teen voting had been defeated, did challenge the act in court. When the case reached the Supreme Court, the justices were sharply divided. After much debate, a majority of five out of nine ruled that Congress could lower the voting age for federal elections but not for local or state elections. This left the states with a big problem: they would have to keep separate voter registration records for federal and local/state elections, a cumbersome and expensive undertaking in the era before everything was computerized, and for general elections there would have to be two separate ballots. Therefore, a constitutional amend-ment—which became the Twenty-sixth Amendment—was quickly pushed through Congress and submitted to the states for ratification. Although some people felt that it was an infringement of states' rights and that states whose voters opposed a lower age limit were being blackmailed, the Twenty-sixth Amendment was ratified in only a hundred days, faster than any other amendment in history, because of the need for time to prepare for the 1972 election.

It was widely believed that the votes of eighteen- to twenty-year-olds would have a major impact on the outcome of elections, beginning with the general election in 1972. Young people's views tended to be liberal, and political analysts predicted that they might even determine who won the presidency. Somewhat to everyone's surprise, this did not happen. Many young people did not bother to vote, and of those who did, most voted the same way as their elders. In 1972 President Richard Nixon, unpopular among the young, was re-elected. In the years since, the only significant difference between age groups has been that fewer young people voted than older people, and until the 2008 election, the percentage of them who did vote consistently declined. In 2008, however, young people voted for President Barack Obama by a larger margin than the rest of the population, but it is too soon to know what that signifies. Did they vote for him on the basis of issues, or because his supporters made an effort to turn out the youth vote, or merely because he is relatively young?

The only conflict that has arisen from the lowering of the voting age has occurred in college towns. Residents of towns where students outnumber homeowners have been upset by the possibility that mere temporary residents would control local politics, or at the very least pass ballot measures in which they had no long-term stake. Therefore, there have sometimes been attempts to prevent students from voting in such towns, and many of these cases have gone to court. Strictly speaking, this is not a Twenty-sixth Amendment issue, because some students are over twenty-one, and disputes arose before younger students were added to their number; court decisions have usually been based on the Fourteenth Amendment's equal protection clause, not on the Twenty-sixth. However, the involvement of eighteen- to twenty-years-olds has exacerbated the problem.

Many students are confused as to whether they can legally vote at college, where they currently live, or must get absentee ballots from where their parents live, and people on both sides of the argument have given out misleading information. It is often claimed that the Supreme Court has ruled that students can vote at their college residence. This is not true in a general sense. The Supreme Court, in *Symm v. United States*, merely affirmed summarily (that is, without issuing its own decision) the decision of a lower court that had ruled students in Texas cannot be required to offer more proof of permanent residence than other voting applicants had to. In the first place, because the Supreme Court did not issue an opinion, the decision is not binding on courts outside Texas—though they normally respect it. More significantly, no one, student or not, can vote in any locality without establishing permanent residence there, which requires stating an intent to remain in that locality and renouncing any former residence. Students cannot be denied the right to vote in a town merely because they are students there or live in dormitories, but they must meet the same residence requirements as everybody else. Those requirements are specified by state laws; there is no national standard, because except with respect to the requirements of the Constitution, it is the states, not the federal government, that determine voter qualifications.

There is nothing in the Twenty-sixth Amendment that prevents a state from setting its voting age *below* eighteen. And recently, a movement has begun to extend the franchise to younger teens. Some foresaw this long ago; for example, in

1959 Congressman W.R. Poage declared, "The same hope to secure the votes of these younger citizens that leads to the dropping of the 21 figure will of course lead some future politician to promise to give the vote to citizens of 17, 16 and possibly even less. There has to be a stopping point. There is always going to be pressure to lower the age limit no matter how low it is." This is probably true—in 2004 there was a serious proposal in California to lower it to fourteen. However, many people today believe that sixteen would be the best minimum age. One reason is that they hope to encourage teens to get in the habit of voting before moving away from home for college or a job.

The right to vote is a fundamental one that for many groups has been hard-won. Perhaps knowing something of its history may lead more young people to take advantage of that right.

Chronology

1820

A measure to lower the voting age is defeated two to one at a Missouri state constitutional convention.

1821

At a New York state convention the idea that a man old enough to fight is old enough to vote is debated. After a close vote, the vote is extended only to men over twenty who have performed military service (at this time, other voters over twenty had to be taxpayers).

1867

Several proposals to let eighteen- to twenty-year-olds vote are made after the Civil War, but all are defeated.

1868

The Fourteenth Amendment, which among other things provides that "a state's representation in Congress will be decreased if it keeps male citizens, who are 21 or older, and who have not committed crimes, from voting," is ratified. This provision, aimed at penalizing states that did not allow blacks to vote, is the only place the age of twenty-one appears in the Constitution. It would prevent a state from setting its voting age *higher* than twenty-one (as during the colonial era, some had) although that issue has not arisen.

1939

In June a Gallup poll, in the first recorded public opinion on the issue in the United States, indicates that 17 percent of the people favored lowering the voting age to eighteen.

1941

Senator Harley Kilgore introduces a constitutional amendment to lower the voting age, on which no action is taken.

On December 7 America enters World War II, during which wide support for lowering the voting age develops.

1942

On October 19, Senator Arthur Vandenberg introduces a Senate resolution proposing a constitutional amendment to lower the voting age to eighteen. The next day, Representative Jennings Randolph introduces a similar one in the House. In January 1943, Vandenberg and Randolph introduce them again. During the next quarter-century other members of Congress introduce such resolutions, and many express support for them, but all stall in committee.

1942–1944

More than forty resolutions to lower the voting age are introduced in thirty-one states, but all are defeated except in Georgia. On August 23, 1943, Georgia lowers its voting age to eighteen.

The National Education Association (NEA) strongly supports a lower voting age, which it believes would add to the significance of social studies in high schools. Public support, as indicated by Gallup polls, rises steadily, reaching 52 percent in September of 1944.

1943

On January 21, First Lady Eleanor Roosevelt writes in her newspaper column, "If young men of eighteen and nineteen are old enough to ... fight their country's battles ... I think we must accept the fact that they are also old enough to know why we fight this war. If that is so, then they are old enough to take part in the political life of their country and to be full citizens with voting powers."

1944

Both major parties consider making the lowering of the voting age a plank in their platforms for the presidential election. Thomas Dewey, the Republican candidate, declines to do so because polls show that 60 percent of potential young voters favor Franklin D. Roosevelt, the Democratic incumbent.

1950–1953

Support for lowering the voting age gains ground during the Korean War but many more state and congressional proposals to do so fail to pass. In 1951 a bill is introduced in Congress to extend voting rights to all members of the armed forces, regardless of age, but it is not passed either.

1952

In January presidential candidate Dwight D. Eisenhower tells reporters, "I believe if a man is old enough to fight he is old enough to vote." Candidate Adlai Stevenson, told of Eisenhower's advocacy, replies, "We had that 18-year-old plan in our platform in Illinois in 1948. I was for it then; I am for it now."

1954

On January 7, President Eisenhower endorses the lowering of the voting age in his State of the Union address. (On January 6, 1956, he does so again.)

On May 21, a resolution to lower the voting age proposed by Senate Judiciary Committee chairman William Langer is voted on by the Senate—the only such resolution to get out of committee prior to 1970. It fails to received the two-thirds majority required for it to pass.

1955

On March 22, the state of Kentucky lowers its voting age to eighteen.

Between 1955 and 1959, thirty-nine states introduce more than ninety proposals into their legislatures to enfranchise men and women under the age of twenty-one, but all are defeated.

1959

Alaska and Hawaii are admitted to the union with a voting age of nineteen in Alaska and twenty in Hawaii, as set by their state constitutions.

1960–1968

Many more state and congressional proposals for enfranchising youth fail to produce action. In 1963, a report on voter participation commissioned by President Lyndon Johnson recommends that each state should carefully consider lowering the voting age to eighteen. On June 27, in a special message to Congress, Johnson declares, "It is time once more for Americans to measure the constraints of custom and tradition against the compelling force of reason and reality in regard to the test of age."

1968

The Republican Party platform endorses state action to lower the minimum voting age to eighteen, while the Democratic Party platform calls for a constitutional amendment to set a national minimum age of eighteen.

In December college students form the organization LUV (Let Us Vote), which within six weeks expands into a nationwide movement with 327 college chapters and 3,000 high school divisions. The next year its official campaign song, "L.U.V.", performed by recording stars Boyce and Hart, becomes a hit.

1969

On February 5, the Youth Franchise Coalition is formed, composed of some of the nation's most influential civil rights and educational organizations. It engages in lobbying Congress and state legislatures to lower the voting age.

On April 21, the Youth and College Division of the National Association for the Advancement of Colored People holds a National Youth Mobilization to Lower the Voting Age in Washington, D.C.

On August 19, Senator Jennings Randolph and sixty-seven co-sponsors introduce a resolution proposing a constitutional amendment extending the right to vote to citizens eighteen years of age or older.

1970

During the year, five states lower the voting age to nineteen or twenty.

On March 4, in response to a proposal by Senator Edward Kennedy that the voting age could be lowered by statute rather than by constitutional amendment, Senate majority leader Mike Mansfield introduces a rider that does that to a pending bill renewing the Voting Rights Act of 1965, an act dealing mainly with practices that interfere with the registration of black voters.

On March 12, the Senate adopts the Voting Rights Act rider by a vote of 64 to 17. On June 15 the House passes the bill by 272 to 132 votes, with some representatives accepting the rider only in order to get the Voting Rights Act renewed. On June 22, President Richard Nixon signs it, despite his belief that the voting age rider is unconstitutional.

In June the states of Oregon and Texas ask the Supreme Court to declare the voting age provisions of the Voting Rights Act unconstitutional on the grounds it conflicts with their state constitutions, and the U.S. Justice Department files suit against Idaho and Arizona for refusing to comply with the voting age provisions. The Supreme Court reviews these four cases together.

On December 21 the Supreme Court rules five to four in *Oregon v. Mitchell* that the voting age provisions of the Voting Rights Act are valid for federal elections, but not for state and local elections.

1971

On January 25, Senator Jennings Randolph, joined by eighty-six cosponsors, again introduces a resolution proposing a constitutional amendment to lower the voting age. On January 29 a similar resolution is introduced in the House of Representatives.

On March 8, the proposal is approved by the Senate Judiciary Committee, and it is passed by the Senate two days later by a vote of ninety-four to zero.

On March 23, the House bill is approved by a vote of four hundred to nineteen, then tabled when the House endorses the Senate version. The proposed amendment is then sent to the states for ratification. It is ratified by five states, starting with Minnesota, on the same day.

Between March 24 and June 30, thirty-two more states ratify the Twenty-sixth Amendment, although many state legislators believe that it is an infringement of states' rights. It is ratified by North Carolina, which gives it the number required for its adoption, on July 1. Four more states ratify it after that.

In *Bright v. Baesler*, a Kentucky court rules that alleged discrimination against young voters in a college town is based on student status, not age, and so the case must be decided on equal protection grounds rather than on the basis of the Twenty-sixth Amendment.

In *Jolicoeur v. Mihaly*, a California court rules that a state law creating a presumption that an unmarried student's residence is his or her parents' home violates the Fourteenth and Twenty-Sixth Amendments.

1972

The first presidential election in which eighteen- to twenty-year-olds can participate is held in November. Over 11 million of them are eligible, but only 48 percent of them vote.

1973

In *Whatley v. Clark* the Fifth Circuit Court rules that a Texas law creating a presumption that students are transient and requiring them to prove otherwise is unconstitutional under the Equal Protection Clause.

1978

In *United States v. Texas* a federal court prohibits a Texas county registrar from requiring student applicants for voter registration to complete a questionnaire that is not required of other applicants, ruling that this violates the Twenty-sixth Amendment.

1979

In *Symm v. United States* the Supreme Court summarily affirms the ruling in *United States v. Texas*.

1986

In *Williams v. Salerno* the U.S. Second Circuit Court rules that a state cannot have a per se rule against registering voters who reside in student dormitories.

2003

A proposal to place a measure lowering the voting age to sixteen on the ballot in Alaska fails by one vote.

2004

A proposal to lower the voting age to seventeen is introduced in the Minnesota legislature but fails to pass.

A bill to lower the voting age to fourteen is introduced in the California legislature, proposing that the votes of fourteen- and fifteen-year-olds count as a quarter of a vote, and those of fifteen- and sixteen-year-olds would count as half a vote. It is rejected.

2005

A voting age of sixteen is proposed for Berkeley, California, city elections, but fails by one vote because of three abstentions.

2008

In twelve states seventeen-year-olds are allowed to vote in primary elections if they will be eighteen by the time of the general election.

A proposal for an Illinois constitutional amendment to lower the voting age to seventeen passes committee by a five-to-three vote and will be considered by the full legislature.
Proposals to lower the voting age to sixteen are pending in several states.

More young people between eighteen and twenty-nine vote in the presidential election than in any previous one, and they favor Barack Obama by a larger margin than any other age group. Some analysts believe this may have been a key factor in his victory.

Historical Background on the Twenty-sixth Amendment

Lowering the Voting Age
Was Not a New Idea

Thomas H. Neale

Thomas H. Neale is an analyst in the American National Government Division of the Library of Congress. In the following excerpt from a report prepared for the Congressional Research Service, he explains the gradual expansion of the right to vote in America. In the early years of the nation, only a small percentage of the population could vote: white males twenty-one years of age or older who owned land or had income above a certain level. During the first half of the nineteenth century, property and income qualifications were eliminated by all states except those that linked voting to tax payment. After the Civil War, the right to vote was extended to blacks by the Thirteenth Amendment to the Constitution. Women did not receive the vote until the passage of the Nineteenth Amendment in 1920. Support for lowering the voting age to eighteen developed during World War II, when the draft age was lowered from twenty to eighteen, and later during the Korean War. Despite many such proposals, however, Congress took no action on them until 1970.

Universal adult suffrage in America has been achieved only after a long series of State and Federal legislative enactments and constitutional amendments. Colonial charters and post-revolutionary State constitutions in many cases established stringent criteria for voting, based on property ownership, level of income, religion, sex, race, and age. Only a very small percentage of the total population, almost without exception white adult males possessing the requisite land holdings or income, qualified to vote.

Thomas H. Neale, *The Eighteen Year Old Vote: The Twenty-Sixth Amendment and Subsequent Voting Rates of Newly Enfranchised Age Groups.* Congressional Research Service, May 20, 1983. http://digital.library.unt.edu/govdocs/crs/permalink/meta-crs-8805:1.

The Philadelphia Constitutional Convention of 1787 chose not to tamper with the existing formulas; it left determination of who had the right to vote in the hands of the States, specifying only that "the Electors [of U.S. representatives] in each State shall have the qualifications requisite for electors of the most numerous Branch of the State Legislature."

Although proposals for popular election of Senators and the President were advanced, the convention effectively removed these offices from direct choice by the people. The Senate was chosen by the legislatures of the States, while the President was chosen by electors in each State appointed "in such manner as the Legislature thereof may direct."

In practice, the right to vote in the early years of the Republic was generally limited to white males 21 years of age or older holding land or possessing a certain level of income or personal property. The electorate was quite small by modern standards. During the first half of the 19th century, however, property and income qualifications were gradually eased. By the time of the Civil War almost all States, save for those linking voting to tax payment, offered universal white manhood suffrage. Rhode Island alone retained a property requirement.

Extending the Vote

The first serious Federal effort to expand the right to vote came after the Civil War, in 1865. Three amendments passed during the Reconstruction era sought to extend full citizenship rights to America's recently emancipated black population. The 13th Amendment, ratified in 1865, incorporated emancipation as a part of the Constitution. The 14th, ratified in 1868, guaranteed citizenship, due process and equal protection of the law to "all persons born or naturalized in the United States, and subject to the jurisdiction thereof." The 15th Amendment specifically guaranteed all adult male citizens the right to vote, notwithstanding "race, color, or previous condition of servitude."

Despite these efforts, large scale voting by blacks did not long survive the end of Reconstruction in 1877; blacks, where not discouraged from voting by terror and intimidation, were systematically purged from the rolls by such devices as poll taxes, lengthened residency requirements, "white" primaries, which prohibited black voting in Democratic primary elections, and "grandfather" clauses, which restricted the franchise to those who were registered to vote before adoption of the 14th and 15th Amendments, and their descendents.

Women achieved the right to vote with the ratification of the 19th Amendment in 1920, while the 23rd Amendment established the right of citizens of the District of Columbia to vote for Presidential electors in 1961.

Many hindrances to voting by black citizens were gradually removed by the Civil Rights Acts of 1957, 1960, and 1964 and the Voting Rights Act, originally passed in 1965, amended and extended in 1970, 1975 and 1982. Another constitutional amendment, the 24th, ratified in 1964, prohibited denial of the right to vote because of failure to pay a poll tax. It could be said that by the late nineteen sixties, proposals to grant the right to vote to 18 to 20 year olds came to be viewed by many as a logical extension of the national trend in broadening the franchise.

World War II Proposals

Although proposals to lower the voting age were occasionally offered as far back as the nineteenth century, broad support for a such an extension first developed during the Second World War. At that time of national crisis, Congress sought to meet the growing needs for military personnel by lowering the age at which males were subject to the draft from 20 to 18 years. On November 13, 1942, President Franklin D. Roosevelt signed legislation lowering the draft age. This action provided an impetus to proposals that the voting age be similarly lowered. Senator Harley Kilgore (D-W.Va.) had pioneered in this

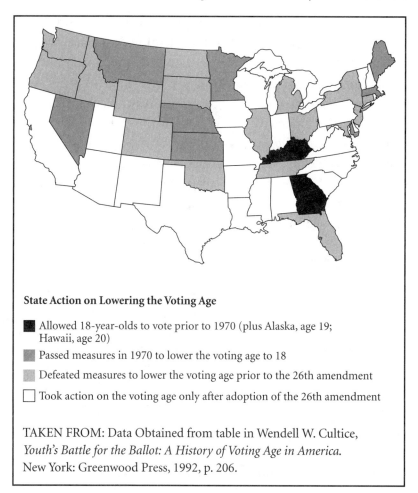

State Action on Lowering the Voting Age

■ Allowed 18-year-olds to vote prior to 1970 (plus Alaska, age 19; Hawaii, age 20)

■ Passed measures in 1970 to lower the voting age to 18

■ Defeated measures to lower the voting age prior to the 26th amendment

☐ Took action on the voting age only after adoption of the 26th amendment

TAKEN FROM: Data Obtained from table in Wendell W. Cultice, *Youth's Battle for the Ballot: A History of Voting Age in America.* New York: Greenwood Press, 1992, p. 206.

area, offering a voting age amendment in 1941; he was joined by Senator Arthur Vandenberg (R-Mich.) and Representatives Jennings Randolph (D-W.Va.) and Victor Wickersham (D-Okla.), who introduced similar resolutions in the second session of the 77th Congress. Senator Kilgore asserted that nearly 90 percent of the approximately 7,000,000 Americans between 18 and 21 were already contributing to the war effort, either through military service or other forms of war work. The movement adopted the watchword "old enough to fight, old enough to vote."

Early in 1943 [First Lady] Eleanor Roosevelt added her voice to the movement for the 18-year-old vote, while the National Education Association also endorsed the concept.

Although informational hearings were held in the House Judiciary Committee in 1943, no action was taken in Congress on any of the amendments offered in the 77th or later wartime Congresses. There was also considerable exploratory action on the local level which did lead to concrete results in one State: in 1943, voters in Georgia approved a constitutional amendment previously approved by the legislature which lowered the age requirement to 18 years.

Postwar Developments

Despite growing public support for a lowered voting age requirement, Congress failed to pass any of the many proposed amendments during the quarter century following World War II, and, in fact, the question reached the floor of either house only once prior to 1970.

In his 1954 State of the Union Message, President Dwight D. Eisenhower urged Congress "to propose to the States a constitutional amendment permitting citizens to vote when they reach the age of 18." Responding to the President's plea, Senate Judiciary Committee Chairman William Langer (R-N.D.) introduced Senate Joint Resolution 53 in the 83d Congress. Senator Langer's resolution was brought to the floor of the Senate for consideration on May 21, 1954, where a coalition of liberal Democratic and moderate Republican senators supported the proposed amendment but were unable to obtain the required two-thirds majority: S.J. Res. 53 failed of passage by a margin of 34 yeas to 24 nays, with 37 Senators not voting.

Although voting age amendments were introduced in every succeeding Congress, and although extensive hearings were held in the 87th, 90th, and 91st Congresses, nothing was reported from committee prior to the 91st Congress.

There was also considerable action in the States during the nineteen fifties. During the Korean War, the realization that many thousands of young men between the ages of 18 and 21 were serving in combat situations spurred introduction of proposals to lower the voting age. By one account, the legislatures of no fewer than 35 States considered reducing the age requirement between 1950 and 1954. In only three instances, however, were the proposals adopted: in the first, Kentucky voters approved reduction of the age limit to 18 in a November 1955 referendum. Alaska and Hawaii, both of which entered the Union in 1959, set voting age at 19 and 20 respectively, in their State constitutions.

Public Support for Lowering the Age

Throughout the four decades prior to the passage of the 26th Amendment, there was a growth of public support for the idea of an 18-year-old voting age limit, as measured by the Gallup Poll. The question was first asked in 1939, and then repeated at intervals.

On March 30, 1963, President John F. Kennedy issued an executive order establishing the President's Commission on Registration and Voting Participation to investigate the causes of widespread failure to register and vote, and to recommend such reforms as seemed advisable. The Commission's report, submitted to President Lyndon B. Johnson in late 1963, provided further impetus for the 18-year-old vote by recommending, in part, that "each State should carefully consider reducing the minimum voting age to 18."

President Johnson carried this legacy forward in a Special Message delivered June 27, 1968, stating in part that,

> ... it is time once more for Americans to measure the constraints of custom and tradition against the compelling force of reason and reality in regard to the test of age. The hour has come to take the next great step in the march of democracy. We should now extend the right to vote to more

than ten million citizens unjustly denied that right. They are the young men and women of America between the ages of 18 and 23.

Resurgence of the movement to lower the voting age in the nineteen sixties seemed to follow the historical pattern, coming as it did while the United States was engaged in military conflict requiring the induction of large numbers of young men into military service. On this occasion, the claim of young Americans that they deserved the right to vote seemed more compelling in light of growing questions about United States military involvement in Indochina.

Numerous arguments both favoring and opposing extension of the franchise to those between the ages of 18 and 21 were raised during the nearly 30 years the question was at issue. A number of the salient points on both sides were considered in an earlier pro-con analysis and are summarized below.

Arguments in Favor of a Lower Age

1. Young citizens today, in part because of the rising level of education, are better equipped to exercise the right of suffrage than were past generations of youth.

2. The idealism and enthusiasm of youthful voters would have a beneficial influence on the conduct of government.

3. Those who are old enough to fight are old enough to vote. Young men have been eligible for selective service at 18 during World War II, the Korean, and Vietnamese conflicts.

4. In many respects, young citizens are legally considered to be of age and are held responsible for their actions.

5. Participation in politics through exercise of the right to vote is an important part of training young men and women to the duties of responsible citizenship.

6. The limited experience with a lower minimum voting age in Georgia, Kentucky, Alaska, and Hawaii demonstrated that the lower minimum worked satisfactorily. The experience of other nations having an 18-year-old minimum is irrelevant, as these nations have governmental systems quite different from ours.

Arguments in Opposition to a Lower Age

1. Any Federal effort to impose a national age standard on the States would be a violation of States' rights. The framers of the Constitution clearly intended that each State should have control over the conditions of voting within its jurisdiction.

2. In general, young people between the ages of 18 and 21 lack the maturity and experience that the exercise of the right to vote demands in a free society.

3. Most other democratically governed nations also have a minimum age requirement of at least 21 years. Some have even higher requirements.

4. The argument that those old enough to fight are old enough to vote is specious [seemingly correct, but not really so]. Physical maturity is quite different from social and political maturity.

5. Lowering the voting age would confer political rights and responsibilities upon minors, persons not generally considered to be legally responsible for their actions.

6. The voting booth ought not to be considered a training ground for citizenship. The right to vote should be restricted to those who are mature enough to assume the full responsibilities of citizenship.

7. Lowering the voting age would cause a flood of student votes in university communities, overwhelming the local electors and substituting for their judgment the opinions

of temporary residents who have nothing material at stake, and whose decisions are less the result of sober consideration of policy alternatives than that of peer group pressures.

Young People Are Mobilizing to Demand the Vote

Susan H. Carter

Susan H. Carter, a journalist for the Massachusetts newspaper the Lowell Sun, *describes the national youth movement known as LUV, short for Let Us Vote. The group was started in December 1968 by a student at the University of the Pacific in Stockton, California, and as of June 1969, when Carter is writing, had established chapters at more than three thousand high schools and four hundred colleges. Spokespersons from LUV chapters appeared before lawmaking groups in many states and in Washington. Carter writes that the group expects some states to lower the voting age soon and hopes that this will put pressure on Congress to lower it nationally within five years. She notes that it is planning a major publicity drive during which comedian Joey Bishop will be promoting the group on his television show and radio stations will be playing the song "LUV" by recording artists Tommy Boyce and Bobby Hart.*

More and more of the 12 million young people in the U.S. between 18 and 21 are beginning to find a fond spot in their hearts for a group called LUV.

Comedian Joey Bishop may be its honorary chairman, but LUV is certainly no laughing matter.

LUV means Let Us Vote. And the public support of the nationwide movement to lower the voting age to 18 is growing daily.

Former President Johnson, President Nixon and 43 senators—from both sides of the political fence—favor lowering the voting age as well as do 65 per cent of the American people, according to polls.

LUV was started last December [1968] by Dennis M. Warren, a 21-year-old pre-law junior at the University of the Pacific [in Stockton, California,] after a speech by Sen. Birch Bayh, D.-Ind. Sen. Bayh spoke on campus for 20 minutes about election reforms, then suggested his student audience do something about extending the vote to 10 year olds.

Dennis and a few of his friends gathered around and decided to pick up the challenge. "'LUV'—a little hokey," Dennis admits with a laugh, "just came up in conversation. Then somebody suggested if we got somebody like Joey Bishop, the movement might really get off the ground."

The question was posed through Jim Mahoney and Associates who handle public relations for the comedian. After he was convinced LUV really was on the level, Joey was enthusiastic and gladly became honorary chairman. He asked Dennis to be on his television show.

That was the start.

Now, LUV has established chapters at 3000 high schools and 400 colleges in 50 states. Dennis has testified before Congressional committees and state legislative committees. Spokesmen from LUV chapters have appeared before lawmaking groups from Washington to California and from Massachusetts to Florida.

Just Beginning

"It's really just beginning," says Dennis. The nationwide group will also be concentrating on radio advertising and spreading their message on talk shows and local television. The United States Information Agency has just completed a 10-minute special news report on LUV. It's in 17 languages and will go to 53 countries.

Dennis Warren is well qualified to spearhead the drive. The dark-haired, articulate young man with a penchant for conservative suits is a former national Pi Kappa Delta [fraternity] debating champion. He has traveled widely with the

A young woman holds a sign that reads, "Give us liberty or give us death! Pass the 26th Amendment!" at an Equal Rights demonstration, 1970s. Hulton Archive/Getty Images.

school's debating team and still does; in one year he logged 40,000 flight miles. He was such an accomplished debater that he even taught a speech course in summer school at the University. (With LUV he's already made six trips to the East Coast so far.)

"The traditionally legal voting age of 21 was established during the Middle Ages at the time when one was eligible for membership in the Knights of the Round Table in accord with one's physical maturity," Dennis writes in a LUV position paper.

"Rather than choosing an age when one was psychologically and mentally prepared to meet the demands of an adult society, our Anglo-Saxon forefathers chose an age based on purely physical criteria. While this may have been a sufficient standard for the Knights of the Round Table, it is both irrelevant and inequitable for men of the 20th Century.

"We cannot adhere to ox-cart standards in the space age."

What the movement is up against is essentially the same old feeling that 18-year-olds simply aren't mature enough to vote.

"I think we'll have it from the federal government in five years," Dennis says confidently and predicts that "several" states will let 18 year olds vote in 1970. So far, eight states are committed to putting the question on the ballot at that time for the voters to consider. (Four states presently allow voting before age 21: Kentucky and Georgia, 18; Alaska, 19; and Hawaii, 20).

One historical fact LUV likes to point out is that as early as 1619, 17 year olds were allowed to cast their ballots for the Virginia House of Burgesses, the nation's first legislative body.

"The action of the states will put a lot of pressure on Congress," Dennis declares.

Organization Growing

The organization is growing in many ways, Dennis is off just about every week-end on speaking engagements, trying to start new chapters and drumming up support from politicians and youth clubs. LUV was 'swamped' with mail after Dennis appeared on Joey Bishop's TV show, and mail still pours in at the rate of 100 to 200 letters a day. Headquarters, which were temporarily housed in the University's student government offices, grew so big they had to move three blocks off campus into a former beauty salon. The rent is donated by the owner, a LUV supporter.

"We got one letter the other day," Dennis says with a grin, "from a guy who said he didn't believe 10 year olds should get to vote but he approved of the way we were going about it. He enclosed two dollars."

In the ensuing months LUV will be even busier and Dennis believes a lot of minds will be changed in the "next six months."

LUV has recently merged part of its efforts with groups such as the National Student Association, the NAACP [National Association for the Advancement of Colored People] and the AFL-CIO [American Federation of Labor and Congress of Industrial Organizations] to form a powerful, national voting-age lobby. There will be big publicity drives. Young people will be at shopping centers selling LUV buttons for 25 cents and pushing LUV bumper stickers and sweatshirts.

Radio stations will be playing the single "LUV," by recording artists Tommy Boyce and Bobby Hart. And Joey Bishop will be periodically reporting LUV's new chapters on a huge map he has on his ABC television program.

"I think it's safe to say," says Dennis Warren, "that LUV has caught the imagination of a lot of the public."

Teen Voting Would Accelerate Undesirable Changes in the Democratic Process

William G. Carleton

William G. Carleton was a professor emeritus of political science at the University of Florida when he wrote the following article, in which he argues that the voting age should not be lowered. In the past, he points out, young people worked, served in the military, and married at much younger ages than they do now, yet the voting age was kept at twenty-one because it was felt that responsibilities requiring thought and judgment demand more maturity than does physical action. Although young people are now better educated, academic education is a vicarious rather than actual experience, and the latter can be gained only by contact with the world through active participation in an occupation or profession. Moreover, the democratic process is changing from grass roots discussion to mere influence by mass media, and late adolescents are the ones most impressed by passing trends and celebrity cults. They do not, in his opinion, have the experience or historical perspective needed to make comparative judgments about social values.

There is growing agitation in the United States to reduce the beginning voting age from the traditional twenty-one years to eighteen years. Four states have lowered the voting age; several states are debating the proposal; the President and important leaders in Congress are advocating it as a national practice; and the opinion polls show a sizeable majority in its favor.

It is curious how few voices, conservative or liberal, have been raised against this mounting movement to enfranchise

William G. Carleton, "Votes for Teen-Agers," *Yale Review*, vol. LVIII, October 1968, pp. 149, 151, 153, 155, 157, 159. Copyright © 1968 Yale University. Reproduced by permission of Blackwell Publishers.

the upper-age adolescents. A notable exception is [President] Harry Truman. Truman, with characteristic practicality and saltiness, has expostulated that it would make more sense to raise the voting age to twenty-five than to lower it to eighteen. Some will shrug off Truman as an old fogey, but his fidelity to our democratic process is unquestionable.

According to the immemorial custom of the English common law, a person reached his majority at the age of twenty-one. This became the voting age in countries inheriting British institutions, and it also became the voting age in most other countries. This has stood for generation after generation. It is strange that now, when the adolescence of youngsters is prolonged far beyond what it was in past times, there should suddenly appear a formidable agitation to enfranchise the late teen-agers.

Actually a reduction in the voting age would have made much more sense in the past than it does today. During the eighteenth and through much of the nineteenth century, young people matured earlier. Boys became subject to the militia and to public road work at the age of sixteen, and some were even graduated from college at that age. They frequently married at seventeen, and the common age was eighteen. Girls married even earlier. An unmarried girl was a 'stale maid' at twenty and a 'thornback' at twenty-five. Young people commonly went to work at fifteen and sixteen, and the hard realities of making a living forced them at an early age to come to grips with the actual world, formulate personal values rooted in it, and become aware of their interests within the social framework.

Yet despite this early maturing, generation after generation allowed the voting age to stand at twenty-one. It was agreed that while the physical duties of citizenship, such as soldiering, road work, joining a sheriff's posse, should be undertaken at an earlier age, those responsibilities requiring thought and judgment, like voting and holding public office, should be postponed to a later time.

The present agitation to enlarge the voting population differs markedly from the many campaigns of the past century and a half to expand the franchise. These past campaigns sought to extend voting privileges to a larger number of adults. These succeeded, and gradually the religious, property, racial, and sex barriers to adult voting fell. All the reform movements in American history—the Jeffersonian, the Jacksonian, the Abolitionist, the Radical Reconstruction, the Populist, the Progressive, the New Deal—sought significant governmental changes, and frequently an extension of the franchise. However, in the past no democratic agitation or movement in America ever advocated a lowering of the voting age to include non-adults.

It is estimated that by 1970 more than 50 per cent of the American population will consist of persons twenty-five years of age or younger. This means that the proportion of voters from the ages of twenty-one to twenty-five will be larger than in the past. For a nation which has always been over-impressed with youth, this greater numerical and voting strength of the youthful population promises in itself to work a distortion. Now, on top of this, comes the agitation deliberately to weight the scales still further in favor of youth by enfranchising the late teen-agers.

Americans Worship Youth

Why has this proposal won such a large popular support at this time?

For one thing, Americans worship youth. They have always done so. (Over a century ago Nathaniel Hawthorne noted repeatedly in his journal of personal experiences in England that while Englishmen accepted age with good grace, the Americans resorted to every contrivance to appear young.) For a number of reasons, middle-aged Americans of this century are better able to retain the feeling and appearance of youth much longer than were the Americans of a century ago.

Today, Americans have created an image which blurs the differential between the chronologically young and middle-aged, and hence they envisage the enfranchisement of the eighteen-year-olds with no sense of shock.

For another thing, Americans are a little conscience-stricken about drafting their youth for military service, particularly for the war in Vietnam. The contrast between the comfortable, even luxurious, life of American civilians and the hard life of draftees in Vietnam is a glaring one. Many Americans have nagging doubts about the national need for the sacrifices in Vietnam. Hence, as a kind of atonement, a large number have come to feel emotionally that 'if they are old enough to fight they are old enough to vote.'

For still another thing, Americans today place an inordinate faith in formal education. Our schools from the kindergarten to the graduate levels seem vastly improved over what they were formerly, and a far larger percentage of our young people attends school at all levels. Besides, many of the oldsters, baffled by the complexities of our technological society, feel that the youngsters, having grown up in that society, necessarily must understand its problems better than the older generations. Hence there is a tendency to equate contemporary political understanding with having been born into the technological society and having had longer and better formal educations. The unsophisticated [people] commonly remark that 'kids go to school longer than they used to,' that they are 'better educated,' that they 'know more,' that they are 'smarter' than their parents and grandparents were at the age of eighteen.

The Military Argument

Just how valid is the cliché that youths old enough to fight are old enough to vote? It certainly carried little weight with prior generations.

Armies in the eighteenth and nineteenth centuries contained a relatively larger number of teen-agers than armies of the twentieth century. Boys often joined the armies at sixteen and seventeen, and some even younger managed in one way or another to slip into the military services. These youngsters could perform certain tasks of agility, like climbing poles and scaling walls, even better than the twenty-one-year-olds. But it was never inferred that because the teen-agers were superior in certain physical feats they should be called on to make decisions.

If ever a generation of fighting men earned the right to vote because of invaluable service to the Nation, it was those youths who fought the American Civil War from 1861 to 1865, a large number of whom were under twenty-one. In many ways the Nation poured out its gratitude to these lads. They were an appealing lot, too, as the war diaries and letters reveal. Compared with the present generation of youth, they were more bucolic [rural], their speech was more colorful and metaphorical, their verbal obscenities were wider in range, more discriminating, and more vivid in imagery. Many of these boys were illiterate, and most of them were semi-literate. But the Americans of earlier generations were not so painfully genteel as we have become today; they did not make the mistake of equating literacy with common sense and political insight. It was, therefore, not fear of illiteracy or semi-literacy that deterred the Civil War generation from giving the ballot to the late teen-agers; it was instead the universal conviction that boys did not become men until the age of twenty-one, that youths below that age, whether literate or illiterate, were simply not mature enough to vote.

The military argument for enfranchising the upper-age adolescents is indeed belated. Future wars, if the *pax atomica* [peace through nuclear deterrence] does not eventually eliminate war itself, will be fought more and more by machines and technicians and less and less by the untrained youths who largely composed the armies of the past. And the technicians, because of the nature of their training, will be old enough to vote anyway.

The Education Argument

An infinitely larger number of young people finish high school and attend college than formerly. Does this better prepare them to participate in politics at an earlier age?

Most young people are flocking to the colleges to prepare themselves for a vocational specialty. The specialties themselves are becoming narrower and more highly technical. Among technicians there are likely to be as many gullible people in matters political as among those who never go to college at all. True, along their educational way most students are exposed to some courses in the social studies and the humanities. But even the social studies are becoming behavioral sciences providing tools for specialists, and the increasing emphasis on 'tooling' reflects itself even in courses for high school and undergraduate college students. Even the old humane liberal arts courses are increasingly emphasizing methodology, quantification, and techniques. (In a recent college lecture trip across the country, the most common complaint I heard from faculty members about the intellectual habits of contemporary students was that the young people today have a passion for immediacy, an impatience with historical perspective. As one faculty member put it: 'This is the generation without a sense of history.') The younger generation is undoubtedly being better trained, but is it being better educated?

Leaving aside this question—whether the humanities and social studies are being better or worse taught than formerly—a larger question remains. Preparation for politics by way of the schools is a vicarious rather than an actual experience; and does vicarious experience, among those too young to have had much experience in actual life, really 'take'? Does not one's awareness of community and individual interests come largely out of direct worldly contacts, active participation in an occupation or profession, and family responsibilities?

High school seniors and college freshmen and sophomores are in age groups from seventeen to twenty. These respond to courses in the social studies and humanities in various ways. In all candor, the response of most is largely routine, ranging from mild and passive interest to indifference to boredom. A minority is genuinely interested in materials dealing with human and social relations, and a few within this minority become deeply attached to them. Their minds seethe and they experience real intellectual ferment. Their involvement, however, is mostly intellectual—not practical, immediate, or applicable. They are still examining, exploring, experimenting. They are often devastatingly critical or given to passing enthusiasms and causes. They are preparing themselves for a larger and enriched view of life, but they have not yet come to settled convictions or a consciousness of their true interests. These will come later when they have had larger experiences in the actual world. It is at this later time that their earlier vicarious experience in school and college courses will pay off and allow them to see their values and their interests with more insights and in larger perspective. Finally, there is another group, the smallest of all, composed of students who have already arrived at rather mature notions of society and of their prospective personal involvement in it. . . .

The Changing Democratic Process

Up until several decades ago, the democratic process in the United States worked much as it had done during the nineteenth century. In the main (despite some serious voting inequities, unfair pressures, intimidation, and manipulation), the process was still a spontaneous and deliberative one. Voters listened to the candidates in person at the courthouse squares and the local opera houses, discussed and debated specific issues, and gave great attention to the views of neighbors who had especially apt insights into politics. The latter, known to keen observers as the 'natural carriers' of the democratic process at the grass roots, had a flair for applied politics. Many of them were not formally educated; sometimes they were only semi-literate; and they might or might not be party workers and professional politicians themselves. These 'natural carriers' had a canny way of seeing through the façades of the candidates, unmasking them, and pointing out the real interests they served. During the ordinary course of a day, they incidentally conversed with small groups at workshops, corner stores, banks, barber shops, saloons, parks, hotel and theatre lobbies, churchyards, lodges, granges; and labor unions; and they more or less dominated the political discussions. . . .

Today our democratic process is coming to operate in a different manner. Voters no longer gather at the courthouse and opera house to listen to a candidate for high public office discuss in detail his position on concrete issues. When they see a candidate in person, they usually get only a fleeting glimpse of him at a supermarket or hear a brief, canned, cliché-ridden talk by a weary, punch-drunk man trying to make thirty or forty personal appearances in a day. When they see him on television, what they are likely to get is a carefully contrived speech written by ghost writers and public relations experts, tailored to appeal to all shades of the public-opinion spectrum and to create an 'image.' In political campaigns today, the voter is bombarded from all sides with a barrage of quick image-builders—flamboyant billboards, newspaper advertisements which exploit stereotypes, spot radio and television commercials which reduce issues to slogans.

What of the neighborhood carrier of the democratic process? He has less and less opportunity to be heard because of the decline of the neighborhood community. People are too busy traveling to and fro in their automobiles for leisurely discussions of politics at street corners; they do their banking at drive-in windows, their eating at drive-in restaurants, their movie-viewing at drive-in theatres; parks are deserted and the word 'park' has come to mean a place to leave a car; people no longer idle in churchyards and barber shops; they no longer gather at folksy lodge meetings as they once did; hotels and motels design tiny lobbies to discourage 'loafers'; and the cold and impersonal cocktail lounges of today are television-ridden and so dimly lighted that one can scarcely see his neighbor at the next bar stool. Leisure is largely reserved for the nightly session with the living-room television set. Besides, who wants to listen to a local political wiseacre when he can tune in on a national television chain and hear a 'big shot'?

In short, our democratic process is becoming less neighborly, less spontaneous, and less autonomous; and more other-directed, more centralized, and more managed and manipulated by the mass media.

Teenagers Are Impressionable

Now, what has all this got to do with voting by the upper-age teensters? Simply this—that while the whole population moves to a more other-directed society, it is the adolescents, the late adolescents, and the post-adolescents who are most impressed by passing trends, by the 'in' thing of the moment, and by 'name,' fame, glamor, and the celebrity cult. . . .

Extremist movements and spectacular 'waves of the future' depend a great deal on their capacity to attract the young—witness Communist leagues, Mussolini's black shirts, Hitler's 'armed bohemians,' Castro's fidelistas, Pan-Africa's black racists, black power's young hotspurs, Mao's Red Guards. Any extremist movement in the United States, if underlying conditions were ripe, would likely draw on a large number of our youths, not a majority but probably enough to threaten an ignition of converging combustible social materials.

Our age is turbulent, volatile, revolutionary. We move with unprecedented swiftness to a technicological, mass-manipulated society. Young people are the most susceptible to the arts of mass management. They have neither the worldly experience nor the historical perspective to make comparative judgments about social values. Hence it is curious that the movement to enfranchise the eighteen-year-olds has not been subjected to more widespread and searching examination. . . .

The basic difficulty is that the public questions on which the electorate today must pass are so complex, even when they involve one's closest individual and group values and interests, that in order to understand them one, must combine personal experience with increasingly larger elements of vicarious experience, that is, second-hand and hearsay evidence derived from reading, and from listening to radio and television. But the voter must already have enough education or other vicarious experience to evaluate intelligently the avalanche of reading and television materials that pours in on him. . . .

Is it not the part of wisdom to attempt to slow down and moderate the palpable trend to the other-directed, non-autonomous, centralized, glamorized, and managed democracy, and whenever and wherever possible to avoid measures (such as the enfranchisement of the immature) which might, however modestly, encourage that trend? Even though today's late teen-agers have had more formal education than most of their elders, the youngsters have not yet assimilated their educational experience; they have not yet discovered their true values and real interests; they have not yet fused their secondary experience with an actual worldly one; and until such fusion is made, vicarious experience is likely to remain experimental, tentative, and untrustworthy.

The Time Has Come to Let Young People Vote

Edward M. Kennedy

Edward M. Kennedy, the brother of President John F. Kennedy, has been a U.S. senator since 1962 and as of 2009 is the second most senior member of the Senate. In the following viewpoint he argues that the voting age should be lowered to eighteen because young people are better informed and more mature than in the past, because allowing them to vote will encourage civic responsibility, and because they already have many rights and responsibilities comparable to voting. He points out that about 30 percent of the armed forces fighting in Vietnam are under twenty-one, and that they deserve the right to vote. Voting is fundamental to the nation's constitutional system, he contends, and the reduction of the voting age should be accomplished by federal action. Although it could be done by a constitutional amendment, in Kennedy's opinion Congress has the power to do it by merely passing a law, and as this would be a much faster method, he believes it should be used.

The time has come to lower the voting age to 18 in the United States, and thereby to bring our youth into the mainstream of the political process. I believe this is the most important single principle we can pursue as a Nation if we are to succeed in bringing our youth into full and lasting participation in our institutions of democratic government.

Members of the Senate are well aware of the many substantial considerations supporting the proposal to lower the voting age to 18 in the United States.

First, our young people today are far better equipped to make the type of choices involved in voting than were past

Edward M. Kennedy, "Should Congress Lower the Voting Age to 18? Pro," *Congressional Digest*, May 1970.

generations of youth. Because of the enormous impact of modern communications, especially television, our youth are extremely well informed on all the crucial issues of our time, foreign and domestic, national and local, urban and rural. Today's 18-year-olds possess far better education than former generations. Our 18-year-olds, for example, have unparalleled opportunities for education at the high school level. Our 19- and 20-year-olds have significant university experience in addition to their high school training. Indeed, in many cases, 18- to 21-year-olds already possess a better education than a large proportion of adults among our general electorate.

Moreover, 18-year-olds today are a great deal more mature and more sophisticated than former generations at the same stage of development. Indeed, through issues like Vietnam and the quality of our environment, and through their participation in programs like the Peace Corps and VISTA [Volunteers in Service to America], our youth have taken the lead on many important questions. They have set a far-reaching example of insight and commitment for us to emulate.

Obviously, the maturity of 18- to 21-year-olds varies from person to person, just as it varies for all age groups in our population. However, on the basis of our broad experience with 18- to 21-year-olds as a class, I believe they possess the requisite maturity, judgment, and stability for responsible exercise of the franchise.

Encourage Civic Responsibility

Second, by lowering the voting age to 18, we will encourage civic responsibility at an earlier age, and thereby promote greater social involvement and political participation for our youth.

In 1963, President Kennedy's Commission on Registration and Voting Participation expressed its deep concern over the low voting participation in the 21–30-year-old bracket. It attributed this low participation to the fact that: 'by the time

Senator Edward Kennedy gives a speech in front of a statue of his brother, President John F. Kennedy. He was a supporter of lowering the voting age to eighteen, which was adopted in 1971. © Bettmann/Corbis.

they have turned 21 . . . many young people are so far removed from the stimulation of the educational process that their interest in public affairs has waned. Some may be lost as voters for the rest of their lives.'

We know that there is already a high incidence of political activity today on campuses and among young people generally, even though they do not have the franchise. None of us who has visited a high school or college in recent years can fail to be impressed by their knowledge and commitment.

I do not agree with the basic objection raised by some that the recent participation of students in violent demonstrations shows that they lack responsibility for mature exercise of the franchise. Those who have engaged in such demonstrations represent only a small percentage of our students. It would be extremely unfair to penalize the vast majority of students because of the reckless conduct of the few.

I believe that both the exercise of the franchise and the expectation of the franchise provide a strong incentive for greater political involvement and understanding. By lowering the minimum voting age to 18, we will encourage political activity not only in the 18- to 21-year-old group, but also in the pre-18-year-old age group as well. Through extension of the franchise, therefore, we will enlarge the meaning of participatory democracy in our society. We will give our youth a new arena for their idealism, activism, and energy.

Third, 18-year-olds already have many rights and responsibilities in our society comparable to voting. It does not automatically follow of course—simply because an 18-year-old goes to war, or works, or marries, or makes a contract, or pays taxes, or drives a car, or owns a gun, or is held criminally responsible like an adult—that he should thereby be entitled to vote. Each right or responsibility in our society presents unique questions dependent on the particular issue at stake. Nonetheless, the examples I have cited demonstrate that in many important respects and for many years, we have conferred far-reaching rights on our youth, comparable in substance and responsibility to the right to vote. Can we really maintain that it is fair to grant them all these rights, and yet withhold the right that matters most, the right to participate in choosing the government under which they live?

Old Enough to Fight, Old Enough to Vote

The well-known proposition—"old enough to fight, old enough to vote"—deserves special mention. To me, this part of the argument for granting the vote to 18-year-olds has great appeal. At the very least, the opportunity to vote should be granted as a benefit in return for the risks an 18-year-old is obliged to assume when he is sent off to fight for his country. About 30 per cent of our forces in Vietnam are under 21. Over 19,000, or almost half of those who have died in action there, were under 21. Can we really maintain that these young men did not deserve the right to vote?

To be sure, as many critics have pointed out, the abilities required for good soldiers are not the same abilities required for good voters. Nevertheless, I believe that we can accept the logic of the argument without making it dispositive.

In the course of the recent hearings I conducted on the draft, I was deeply impressed by the conviction and insight that our young citizens demonstrated in their constructive criticism of our present draft laws. There are many issues in the 91st Congress and in our society at large with comparable relevance and impact on the Nation's youth. They have the capacity to counsel us wisely, and they should be heard at the polls.

Fourth, our present experience with voting by persons under 21 justifies its extension to the entire Nation. Lowering the voting age will improve the overall quality of our electorate, and will make it more truly representative of our society.

I have already stated my feeling that 18- to 21-year-olds possess adequate maturity for responsible use of the franchise. Equally important, by adding our youth to the electorate, we will gain a group of enthusiastic, sensitive, idealistic and vigorous new voters.

I am aware that many arguments have been advanced to prevent the extension of the franchise to 18-year-olds. It may be that the issue is one—like woman suffrage in the early nineteen hundreds—that cannot be finally resolved by reason or logic. Attitudes on the question are more likely to be determined by an emotional or a political response. It is worth noting, however, that almost all of the arguments now made against extending the franchise to 18-year-olds were also made against the 19th Amendment, which granted suffrage to women. Yet, no one now questions the wisdom of that Amendment.

There is, of course, an important political dimension to 18-year-old voting. The enfranchisement of 18-year-olds would add approximately ten million persons to the voting age population in the United States. It would increase the eligible electorate in the Nation by slightly more than 8 per cent. If there were dominance of any one particular party among this large new voting population, or among sub-groups within it, there might be an electoral advantage for that party or its candidates. As a result, 18-year-old voting would become a major partisan issue, and would probably not carry in the immediate future. For my part, I believe that the risk is extremely small. Like their elders, the youth of America are of all political persuasions. The Nation as a whole would derive substantial benefits by granting them a meaningful voice in shaping their future.

The Right to Vote Is Fundamental

The right to vote is the fundamental political right in our constitutional system. It is the cornerstone of all other basic rights. It guarantees that our democracy will be government of the people and by the people, not just for the people. By securing the right to vote, we help to insure, in the historic words of the Massachusetts Bill of Rights, that our Government 'may be a government of laws, and not of men.' Millions of young Americans have earned that right, and we must respond.

I believe not only that the reduction of the voting age to 18 is desirable, but also that Federal action is the best route to accomplish the change, and that the preferred method of Federal change should probably be by statute rather than by constitutional amendment.

In the past, I have leaned toward placing the initiative on the States in this important area, and I have strongly supported the efforts being made in many States, including Massachusetts, to lower the voting age by amending the State Constitutions.

Progress on the issue in the States has been significant, even though it has not been as rapid as many of us had hoped. The issue has been extensively debated in all parts of the Nation. Public opinion polls in recent years have demonstrated that a substantial and increasing majority favor extension of the franchise to 18-year-olds.

In light of these important developments, the time is ripe for Congress to play a greater role. Perhaps the most beneficial advantage of action by Congress is that it would insure national uniformity on this basic political issue. Indeed, the possible discrepancies that may result if the issues is left to the States are illustrated by the fact that of those few States which have already lowered the voting age below 21, two—Georgia and Kentucky—have fixed the minimum voting age at 18. The other two—Alaska and Hawaii—have fixed the age at 19 and 20 respectively. Left to State initiative, therefore, the result is likely at best to be an uneven pattern of unjustifiable variation.

Lower the Voting Age by Statute

Federal action on the voting age is therefore both necessary and appropriate. The most obvious method of Federal action is by amending the Constitution, but it is not the only method. I believe that Congress has the authority to act in this area by statute, and to enact legislation establishing a uniform minimum voting age applicable to all States and to all elections, Federal, State and local.

The decision whether to proceed by constitutional amendment or by statute is a difficult one. One of the most important considerations is the procedure involved in actually passing a constitutional amendment by two-thirds of the Congress and three-fourths of the State legislatures. The lengthy delay involved in the ratification process would probably make it impossible to complete the ratification of a constitutional amendment before many years have elapsed.

It is clear that Congress should be slow to act by statute on matters traditionally reserved to the States. Where sensitive issues of great political importance are concerned, the path of constitutional amendment tends to insure wide discussion and broad acceptance at all levels—Federal, State and local—of whatever change eventually takes place. Indeed, at earlier times in our Nation's history, a number of basic changes in voting qualifications were accomplished by constitutional amendment.

At the same time, however, it is worth emphasizing that in more recent years, changes of comparable magnitude have been made by statute, one of the most important of which was the Federal Voting Rights Act of 1965. Unlike the question of direct popular election of the President, which is also now pending before us, lowering the voting age does not work the sort of deep and fundamental structural change in our system of government that would require us to make the change by pursuing the arduous route of constitutional amendment.

Because of the urgency of the issue, and because of its gathering momentum, I believe that there are overriding considerations in favor of Federal action by statute to accomplish the goal. Possibly, it may be appropriate to incorporate the proposal as an amendment to the bill now pending in the Senate to extend the Voting Rights Act. Indeed, if enough support can be generated, it could be possible for 18-year-olds to go to the polls for the first time this fall—November 1970. . . .

The authority of Congress to act by statute is based on Congress' power to enforce the Fourteenth Amendment by whatever legislation it believes is appropriate. To be sure, the Constitution grants primary authority to the States to establish the conditions of eligibility for voting in Federal elections. Under these provisions, the voting qualifications established by a State for members of the most numerous branch of the State legislature also determine who may vote for United States Representatives and Senators.

It has long been clear, however, that a State has no power to condition the right to vote on qualifications prohibited by other provisions of the Constitution, including the Fourteenth Amendment. No one believes, for example, that a State could deny the right to vote to a person because of his race or his religion. . . .

With respect to granting the vote to 18-year-olds, it is enough for Congress to weigh the justifications for and against extending the franchise to this age-group. If Congress concludes that the justification in favor of extending the franchise outweighs the justification for restricting the franchise, then Congress has the power to change the law by statute and grant the vote to 18-year-olds.

A Constitutional Amendment May Not Be Needed to Lower the Voting Age

Fred P. Graham

Fred P. Graham wrote about legal issues for The New York Times *and was the author of several books. In the following article he reports that Congress has added an eighteen-year-old voting age amendment onto the Voting Rights Bill then being considered and that it seems likely to pass. The idea of lowering the voting age was not previously popular in Congress, he says, because amending the Constitution is a slow and cumbersome process. But the picture changed when Senator Edward M. Kennedy began to argue that a constitutional amendment would not be necessary. Kennedy based this argument on a theory that although the states have the authority to set voting qualifications, they may not violate any specific provisions of the Constitution such as the Fourteenth Amendment's prohibition against denial of equal rights, and the Fourteenth Amendment gives Congress the power to enforce those provisions through legislation. The proposed law states that it is discriminatory for states to deny the vote to persons who are old enough to be drafted into the military, and therefore the Supreme Court can be expected to let it stand. Some people, says Graham, believe this would have a major effect on the future balance of power between Congress and the Court. Moreover, he notes, President Richard Nixon contends that doubts about the law's constitutionality might throw the 1972 election into turmoil. But many observers believe the eighteen-year-old voting age is an idea whose time has come.*

The Age of Aquarius [referring to a popular belief, especially among young people, that a New Age was beginning] appears to be overtaking the Constitution over the issue of lowering the voting age to 18 by means of a statute rather than a constitutional amendment.

Until the events or the past few days, when the Senate tacked an 18-year-old vote amendment onto the Voting Rights Bill and the House leadership cleared the way for a vote on the measure after the Easter recess, few persons would have thought that lowering the voting age was likely in the foreseeable future. Yet it now seems altogether possible that the 10 million young people between ages 18 and 21 will be granted the franchise in time to vote in the 1972 Presidential election—and and that in the process a precedent will be set that will streamline the system of constitutional change to meet some of the pressures of the jet age.

All this developed out of an unlikely political and constitutional background.

The idea of lowering the voting age has been a perennial political lemon in Congress, where the "senility system" rewards advanced age with committee chairmanships, the better to bottle up vote reform bills with. Moreover, with youthful protestors in bad odor lately, the 18-year-old-vote idea had been rejected by the voters of more than a half-dozen states in the past two years.

Furthermore, when women were given the vote and when the poll tax was eliminated in national elections, constitutional amendments were considered necessary to make the changes. It was assumed that the same cumbersome process would have to be used to lower the voting age. With a two-thirds vote of both Houses of Congress and ratification by three-fourths of the states needed to amend the Constitution, Congressmen could be cool to the idea without fear that young people would suddenly get the vote and use it against them.

Senate Stampede

This picture changed, almost overnight, when Senator Edward
M. Kennedy and other Democratic liberals began to argue
persuasively that under a novel constitutional theory, the voting age could be quickly lowered by means of a simple statute.

With the prospect looming large that millions of young
people might soon have the vote, there was a stampede in the
Senate to be for it. An amendment lowering the voting age to
18 in all elections was tacked onto the proposed Voting Rights
Act by a 64-to-17 margin, and it was sent to the House, where
its chances are bright.

This remarkable political spasm was an impressive tribute
to the occasional impact of scholarly work on public policy.
Senator Kennedy got the idea originally from a 1966 article in
the *Harvard Law Review* by former Solicitor General Archibald
Cox, who argued as follows:

1. Although the Constitution gives the states the general
   authority to set voting qualifications, they must not violate any specific individual safeguards of the Constitution, such as the 14th Amendment's prohibition against
   state actions that deny persons equal protection of the
   laws.

2. A section of the 14th Amendment gives Congress the
   power to enforce the rights created in the amendment
   "by appropriate legislation."

3. In a historic 1966 decision, *Katzenbach v. Morgan*, the
   Supreme Court held that if Congress acts to enforce the
   14th Amendment by passing a law declaring that a type
   of state law discriminates against a certain class of persons, the Supreme Court will let the law stand if the
   justices can "perceive a basis" for Congress's action.

His conclusion: If Congress declares that state laws that
deny the vote to 18-, 19- and 20-year-olds violate their 14th

Amendment rights, the Supreme Court will uphold the law, because there is a perceptible basis for such a finding of discrimination.

The law now moving through Congress states that it is unfair and discriminatory for the states to deny the vote to persons who are old enough to be drafted to fight for the country—particularly since there is no compelling reason why they shouldn't be allowed to vote.

Opposition by the President

The Nixon Administration is opposing the idea by arguing that such fundamental changes shouldn't be made without the consensus of a constitutional amendment. It also contends that doubts about the law's constitutionality might throw the 1972 election into turmoil.

Cynics have suggested that President Nixon, whose popular vote margin in 1968 was only 224,000 votes, would prefer that 10 million young people not be added to the electorate until after he wins re-election in 1972. They also point out that the Government supports the use of a statute rather than a constitutional amendment to eliminate state residency requirements for voting and voter literacy tests, and that both of these measures are based upon the new 14th Amendment theory.

Many observers feel that the 18-year-old-vote proposal has now become an idea whose time has come, and that the more significant question is what broader implications may arise from the acceptance of this new theory that gives Congress the power to make constitutional changes that used to require constitutional amendments.

Mr. Cox cautioned in his article that the development "would have enormous consequences for the Federal system" by introducing "a strikingly novel form of judicial deference to Congressional power" into our constitutional system. He and many other admirers of the activist Warren Court [the

Supreme Court as led by chief justice Earl Warren] applaud this trend. They hope that it will encourage Congress to enact needed reforms, and relieve the Supreme Court of the temptation to do so itself.

Congress's use of this new power to enfranchise the young is now favored by many liberals, but some liberals are instinctively leery of Congressional power, and there are signs of uneasiness in their ranks about the new trend.

It is being whispered about among liberals that the present exercise might whet Congress's appetite, and that it may soon confront the Supreme Court with laws affecting the rights of criminal suspects and racial minorities that the justices might find objectionable but must uphold because they can "perceive a basis" for what Congress has done.

Changing the Voting Age Will Require a Constitutional Amendment

Richard Nixon

Richard Nixon was the thirty-seventh president of the United States. The following viewpoint is the text of identical letters he wrote to John W. McCormack, the Speaker of the House; Carl Albert, the House majority leader; and Gerald R. Ford, then the House minority leader. In the letter, he states that the question is not whether eighteen-year-olds should be given the vote, but how. In his opinion, it appears that a constitutional amendment could be readily approved, whereas if a law giving them the vote is passed by Congress and later declared unconstitutional by the courts, the effects will be disastrous. It will have raised false hopes among young people, and the outcome of many state and local elections—possibly even the next national election—will be thrown in doubt, leaving not only the presidency but the membership of Congress in question. Nixon argues that the Constitution makes clear that the power to set voter qualifications belongs to the states, and that the voting laws Congress has previously passed involved discrimination against minorities, which is not comparable to setting a voting age applicable to everyone. The age has to be set somewhere, and Congress has no authority to substitute its judgment for that of the states. Furthermore, for it to attempt to do so would result in damaging controversy about whether Congress or the Supreme Court has the last word on such issues.

A constitutional issue of great importance is currently before the House. As you know, the Senate has attached to the bill modifying and extending the Voting Rights Act of

Richard Nixon, "Letter to House Leaders Supporting a Constitutional Amendment to Lower the Voting Age," Public Papers of the Presidents, April 27, 1970. (Washington, D.C.: Government Printing Office, 1956). pp. 401–404.

1965 a rider that purports to enable Americans between the ages of 18 and 21 to vote in Federal, State and local elections.

I say "purports" because I believe it would not in fact confer the vote. I believe that it represents an unconstitutional assertion of Congressional authority in an area specifically reserved to the States, and that it therefore would not stand the test of challenge in the courts. This belief is shared by many of the Nation's leading constitutional scholars.

I strongly favor the 18-year-old vote. I strongly favor enactment of the Voting Rights Bill. But these are entirely separate issues, each of which deserves consideration on its own merits. More important, each needs to be dealt with in a way that is constitutionally permissible—and therefore, in a way that will work.

Because the issue is now before the House, I wish to invite the urgent attention of the Members to the grave constitutional questions involved in the 18-year-old vote rider, and to the possible consequences of ignoring those questions.

Statute vs. Amendment

The matter immediately at issue is not whether 18-year-olds should be given the vote, but how: by simple statute, or by constitutional amendment.

The argument for attempting it by statute is one of expediency. It appears easier and quicker.

The constitutional amendment route is admittedly more cumbersome, but it does appear that such an amendment could be readily approved. A resolution proposing such an amendment already has been introduced in the Senate, sponsored by two-thirds of the members, the same number required for passage. Sentiment in the House seems strongly in favor. Some contend that ratification would be a long and uncertain process. However, public support for the 18-year-old vote has been growing, and certainly the submission to the States of a constitutional amendment, passed by two-thirds of both Houses and endorsed by the President, would provide powerful additional momentum. An historical footnote is pertinent: When the women's suffrage amendment was proposed in 1919, many said the States would never go along—but ratification was completed in less than 15 months.

If the Senate provision is passed by the Congress, and if it is later declared unconstitutional by the courts, it will have immense and possibly disastrous effects.

At the very least, it will have raised false hopes among millions of young people—led by the Congress to believe they had been given the vote, only to discover later that what the Congress had purported to confer was not in its power to give.

It will have cost valuable time, during which a constitutional amendment could have been submitted to the States and the process of ratification gone forward. It would almost certainly mean that the 18-year-old vote could not be achieved before the 1972 election.

Beyond this, there looms the very real possibility that the outcome of thousands of State and local elections, and possibly even the next national election, could be thrown in doubt: because if those elections took place before the process of judicial review had been completed, no one could know for sure whether the votes of those under 21 had been legally cast. It takes little imagination to realize what this could mean. The Nation could be confronted with a crisis of the first magnitude. The possibility that a Presidential election, under our present system, could be thrown into the House of Representatives is widely regarded as dangerous; but suppose that a probably unconstitutional grant of the 18-year-old vote left the membership of the House unsettled as well?

The Senate measure contains a provision seeking an early test of its constitutionality, but there can be no guarantee that such a test would actually be completed before elections took place. And the risk of chaos, if it were not completed, is real.

The Constitutional Questions

On many things the Constitution is ambiguous. On the power to set voting qualifications, however, the Constitution is clear and precise: within certain specified limits, this power belongs to the States. Three separate provisions vest this power with the States: Article I, Section 2 (election of members of the House of Representatives), the Tenth Amendment (reserved powers) and the Seventeenth Amendment (direct election of Senators) all lodge this power with the States. There are four provisions placing limitations on this power: the vote cannot be limited on grounds of race (the Fifteenth Amendment), sex (the Nineteenth Amendment), or failure to pay a poll tax (the Twenty-Fourth Amendment); nor can States impose voting qualifications so arbitrary, invidious or irrational as to constitute a denial of equal protection of the laws (the Fourteenth Amendment).

Advocates of the proposal that passed the Senate rely on the power given Congress under the Fourteenth Amendment to enforce equal protection of the laws, and particularly on the Supreme Court's 1966 decision in the case of *Katzenbach v. Morgan*. This case upheld Federal legislation enfranchising residents of New York who had attended school in Puerto Rico, and who were literate in Spanish but not in English. However, I do not believe that the Court's decision in *Katzenbach v. Morgan* authorizes the power now asserted by the Senate to enfranchise young people. Neither do I believe it follows that because Congress has power to suspend literacy tests for voting throughout the Nation, as the new Voting Rights Act would do, it has power also to decide for the entire Nation what the proper age qualification should be.

Where Puerto Ricans were denied the right to vote, the Court could readily conclude that there had been discriminatory treatment of an ethnic minority. This was especially so because of the particular circumstances of those whose rights were at issue: U.S. citizens by birth, literate in Spanish, but not literate in English because their schools, though under the American flag, had used Spanish as the language of instruction.

Similarly with literacy tests: the Court already has upheld the right of Congress to bar their use where there is presumptive evidence that they have been used in a discriminatory fashion. If Congress now finds that literacy tests everywhere impose a special burden on the poor and on large numbers of black Americans, and for this reason abolishes literacy tests everywhere, it is using the same power which was upheld when the Court sustained the Voting Rights Act of 1965.

To go on, however, and maintain that the 21-year voting age is discriminatory in a constitutional sense is a giant leap. This limitation—as I believe—may be no longer justified, but it certainly is neither capricious nor irrational. Even to set the limit at 18 is to recognize that it has to be set somewhere. A 21-year voting age treats all alike, working no invidious distinction among groups or classes. It has been the tradition in this country since the Constitution was adopted, and it was the standard even before; it still is maintained by 46 of the 50 states; and, indeed, it is explicitly recognized by Section 2 of the Fourteenth Amendment itself as the voting age.

If it is unconstitutional for a State to deny the vote to an 18-year-old, it would seem equally unconstitutional to deny it to a 17-year-old or a 16-year-old. As long as the question is simply one of judgment, the Constitution gives Congress no power to substitute its judgment for that of the states in a matter such as age qualification to vote, which the Supreme Court has recognized is one which the States may properly take into consideration.

One Constitution

A basic principle of constitutional law is that there are no trivial or less important provisions of the Constitution. There are no constitutional corners that may safely be cut in the ser-

President Richard Nixon affixes his signature to signify that he is witness to the certification of ratification of the Twenty-sixth Amendment to the U.S. Constitution, which gives eighteen-year-olds the right to vote, July 1, 1971. © Bettmann/Corbis.

vice of a good cause. The Constitution is indivisible. It must be read as a whole. No provision of it, none of the great guarantees of the Bill of Rights is secure if we are willing to say that any provision can be dealt with lightly in order to achieve one or another immediate end. Neither high purpose nor expediency is a good excuse. We damage respect for law, we feed cynical attitudes toward law, whenever we ride roughshod over any law, let alone any constitutional provision, because we are impatient to achieve our purposes.

To pass a popular measure despite the Constitutional prohibition, and then to throw on the Court the burden of declaring it unconstitutional, is to place a greater strain and burden on the Court than the Founding Fathers intended, or than the Court should have to sustain. To enact the Senate proposal would be to challenge the Court to accept, or to reject, a fateful step in the redistribution of powers and functions, not only between the Federal Government and the States but also between itself and the Congress.

Historically, under the Fourteenth Amendment as well as under many other provisions of the Constitution, it has been the duty of the Court to define and enforce the division of powers between the Federal Government and the States. Section 5 of the Fourteenth Amendment gives Congress power to "enforce" Constitutionally-protected rights against intrusion by the States; but the primary role in defining what those rights are belongs to the Court.

For the most part, the Court has acted with due deference and respect for the views of Congress, and for Congress' assessment of facts and conditions and the needs to which they give rise. But the Court has had the last word.

However, it is difficult to see how the Court could uphold the Senate proposal on the 18-year-vote without conceding that Congress now has the last word.

To present this challenge to the Court would thus raise equal and opposite dangers: on the one hand, if the Court acquiesced, its own power as the protector of our rights could be irreparably diminished; and on the other, if the Court rebuffed the challenge, the often valuable latitude Congress now has under broad readings of its Fourteenth Amendment power might in consequence be severely limited. Neither outcome, in my view, would be desirable.

The Path of Reason

I have recently canvassed many of the Nation's leading constitutional scholars for their views on the Senate proposal. Some feel that, by a broad reading of *Katzenbach v. Morgan*, the proposal's constitutionality could be sustained. The great majority, however, regard it as unconstitutional—and they voice serious concern not only for the integrity of the Constitution but also for the authority of the Court, if it should be sustained.

At best, then, it would be enacted under a heavy constitutional cloud, with its validity in serious doubt. Even those who support the legislation most vigorously must concede the existence of a serious constitutional question.

At worst, it would throw the electoral process into turmoil during a protracted period of legal uncertainty, and finally leave our young people frustrated, embittered and voteless.

I therefore urge:

- That the 18-year-old vote rider be separated from the bill extending the Voting Rights Act.

- That the Voting Rights Bill be approved.

- That Congress proceed expeditiously to secure the vote for the Nation's 18-, 19-, and 20-year-olds in the one way that is plainly provided for in the Constitution, and the one way that will leave no doubt as to its validity: Constitutional amendment.

Constitutional Implications of the New Law

The Voting Rights Act Passed by Congress Is Valid Only for National Elections

Hugo Black

Hugo Black was a justice of the Supreme Court from 1937 until 1971, and he is considered one of the most influential members of the Court in the twentieth century. He believed in a literal interpretation of the Constitution and in the principle that the Bill of Rights was made applicable to the states by the Fourteenth Amendment. The following is the majority opinion he wrote in Oregon v. Mitchell, *which dealt with, among other things, the question of whether Congress had the authority to lower the voting age from twenty-one to eighteen by passing a law. Black explains the Court's decision that the law was valid with respect to federal elections but invalid with respect to state and local elections. Congress had thought that under the equal rights clause of the Fourteenth Amendment, it had the power to strike down state laws denying the vote to young people old enough to serve in the military. Black states, however, that the Fourteenth Amendment was intended only to prevent discrimination on the basis of race, and because the Constitution gives the right to determine voter qualifications to the states, that right cannot be overridden for reasons having nothing to do with race.*

I believe Congress can fix the age of voters in national elections, such as congressional, senatorial, vice-presidential and presidential elections, but cannot set the voting age in state and local elections. . . .

The Framers of our Constitution provided in Art. I, Sec. 2, that members of the House of Representatives should be

Hugo Black, majority opinion, *Oregon v. Mitchell*, U.S. Supreme Court, December 21, 1970.

elected by the people and that the voters for Representatives should have "the Qualifications requisite for Electors of the most numerous Branch of the State Legislature." Senators were originally to be elected by the state legislatures, but, under the Seventeenth Amendment, Senators are also elected by the people, and voters for Senators have the same qualifications as voters for Representatives. In the very beginning, the responsibility of the States for setting the qualifications of voters in congressional elections was made subject to the power of Congress to make or alter such regulations if it deemed it advisable to do so. This was done in Art. I, Sec. 4, of the Constitution, which provides: "The Times, Places and Manner of holding Elections for Senators and Representatives, shall be prescribed in each State by the Legislature thereof; *but the Congress may at any time by Law make or alter such Regulations*, except as to the Places of chusing Senators." (Emphasis supplied.)

Moreover, the power of Congress to make election regulations in national elections is augmented by the Necessary and Proper Clause. In *United States v. Classic* (1941), where the Court upheld congressional power to regulate party primaries, Mr. Justice [Harlan F.] Stone, speaking for the Court, construed the interrelation of these clauses of the Constitution, stating:

> While, in a loose sense, the right to vote for representatives in Congress is sometimes spoken of as a right derived from the states ..., this statement is true only in the sense that the states are authorized by the Constitution to legislate on the subject as provided by Sec. 2 of Art. I, to the extent that Congress has not restricted state action by the exercise of its powers to regulate elections under Sec. 4 and its more general power under Article I, Sec. 8, clause 18 of the Constitution "to make all laws which shall be necessary and proper for carrying into execution the foregoing powers."

The breadth of power granted to Congress to make or alter election regulations in national elections, including the qualifications of voters, is demonstrated by the fact that the Framers of the Constitution and the state legislatures which ratified it intended to grant to Congress the power to lay out or alter the boundaries of the congressional districts. In the ratifying conventions, speakers "argued that the power given Congress in Art. I, Sec. 4, was meant to be used to vindicate the people's right to equality of representation in the House." *Wesberry v. Sanders* (1964), and that Congress would "'most probably . . . lay the state off into districts.'" And in *Colegrove v. Green* (1946), no Justice of this Court doubted Congress' power to rearrange the congressional districts according to population; the fight in that case revolved about the judicial power to compel redistricting.

Surely no voter *qualification* was more important to the Framers than the *geographical qualification* embodied in the concept of congressional districts. The Framers expected Congress to use this power to eradicate "rotten boroughs," and Congress has, in fact, used its power to prevent States from electing all Congressmen at large. There can be no doubt that the power to alter congressional district lines is vastly more significant in its effect than the power to permit 18-year-old citizens to go to the polls and vote in all federal elections.

Congress Can Regulate National Elections

Any doubt about the powers of Congress to regulate congressional elections, including the age and other qualifications of the voters, should be dispelled by the opinion of this Court in *Smiley v. Holm* (1932). There, Chief Justice [Charles E.] Hughes, writing for a unanimous Court, discussed the scope of congressional power under Sec. 4 at some length. He said:

> The subject matter is the "times, places and manner of holding elections for Senators and Representatives." It cannot be

doubted that these comprehensive words embrace authority to provide a complete code for congressional elections, not only as to times and places, but in relation to notices, registration, supervision of voting, protection of voters, prevention of fraud and corrupt practices, counting of votes, duties of inspectors and canvassers, and making and publication of election returns; in short, to enact the numerous requirements as to procedure and safeguards which experience shows are necessary in order to enforce the fundamental right involved. . . .

This view is confirmed by the second clause of Article I, section 4, which provides that "the Congress may at any time by law make or alter such regulations," with the single exception stated. The phrase "such regulations" plainly refers to regulations of the same general character that the legislature of the State is authorized to prescribe with respect to congressional elections. In exercising this power, the Congress may supplement these state regulations or may substitute its own. . . . It "has a general supervisory power over the whole subject."

In short, the Constitution allotted to the States the power to make laws regarding national elections, but provided that, if Congress became dissatisfied with the state laws, Congress could alter them. A newly created national government could hardly have been expected to survive without the ultimate power to rule itself and to fill its offices under its own laws. The Voting Rights Act Amendments of 1970, now before this Court, evidence dissatisfaction of Congress with the voting age set by many of the States for national elections. I would hold, as have a long line of decisions in this Court, that Congress has ultimate supervisory power over congressional elections. Similarly, it is the prerogative of Congress to oversee the conduct of presidential and vice-presidential elections and to set the qualifications for voters for electors for those offices. It cannot be seriously contended that Congress has less power over the conduct of presidential elections than it has over congressional elections.

States Control State Elections

On the other hand, the Constitution was also intended to preserve to the States the power that even the Colonies had to establish and maintain their own separate and independent governments, except insofar as the Constitution itself commands otherwise. My Brother [Justice John Marshall] Harlan as persuasively demonstrated that the Framers of the Constitution intended the States to keep for themselves, as provided in the Tenth Amendment the power to regulate elections. My major disagreement with my Brother Harlan is that, while I agree as to the States' power to regulate the elections of their own officials, I believe, contrary to his view, that Congress has the final authority over federal elections. No function is more essential to the separate and independent existence of the States and their governments than the power to determine, within the limits of the Constitution, the qualifications of their own voters for state, county, and municipal offices and the nature of their own machinery for filling local public offices. Moreover, Art. I, Sec. 2, is a clear indication that the Framers intended the States to determine the qualifications of their own voters for state offices, because those qualifications were adopted for federal offices unless Congress directs otherwise under Art. I, Sec. 4. It is a plain fact of history that the Framers never imagined that the national Congress would set the qualifications for voters in every election from President to local constable or village alderman. It is obvious that the whole Constitution reserves to the States the power to set voter qualifications in state and local elections, except to the limited extent that the people, through constitutional amendments, have specifically narrowed the powers of the States. Amendments Fourteen, Fifteen, Nineteen, and Twenty-four, each of which has assumed that the States had general supervisory power over state elections, are examples of express limitations on the power of the States to govern themselves. And the Equal Protection Clause of the Fourteenth Amendment was never intended to destroy the States' power to govern themselves, making the Nineteenth and Twenty-fourth Amendments superfluous. My Brother [Justice William] Brennan's opinion, if carried to its logical conclusion, would, under the guise of insuring equal protection, blot out all state power, leaving the 50 States as little more than impotent figureheads. In interpreting what the Fourteenth Amendment means, the Equal Protection Clause should not be stretched to nullify the States' powers over elections which they had before the Constitution was adopted and which they have retained throughout our history.

Of course, the original design of the Founding Fathers was altered by the Civil War Amendments and various other amendments to the Constitution. The Thirteenth, Fourteenth, Fifteenth, and Nineteenth Amendments have expressly authorized Congress to "enforce" the limited prohibitions of those amendments by "appropriate legislation." The Solicitor General contends in these cases that Congress can set the age qualifications for voters in state elections under its power to enforce the Equal Protection Clause of the Fourteenth Amendment.

The Fourteenth Amendment

Above all else, the framers of the Civil War Amendments intended to deny to the States the power to discriminate against persons on account of their race. While this Court has recognized that the Equal Protection Clause of the Fourteenth Amendment in some instances protects against discriminations other than those on account of race, it cannot be successfully argued that the Fourteenth Amendment was intended to strip the States of their power, carefully preserved in the original Constitution, to govern themselves. The Fourteenth Amendment was surely not intended to make every discrimination between groups of people a constitutional denial of equal protection. Nor was the Enforcement Clause of the

Fourteenth Amendment intended to permit Congress to prohibit every discrimination between groups of people. On the other hand, the Civil War Amendments were unquestionably designed to condemn and forbid every distinction, however trifling, on account of race.

To fulfill their goal of ending racial discrimination and to prevent direct or indirect state legislative encroachment on the rights guaranteed by the amendments, the Framers gave Congress power to enforce each of the Civil War Amendments. These enforcement powers are broad. In construing Section 5 of the Fourteenth Amendment, the court has stated: "It is not said the *judicial power* of the general government shall extend to enforcing the prohibitions and to protecting the rights and immunities guaranteed. It is not said that branch of the government shall be authorized to declare void any action of a State in violation of the prohibitions. *It is the power of Congress which has been enlarged.*"

Ex parte Virginia (1880) (Emphasis added in part.) And in *South Carolina v. Katzenbach* (1966), the Court upheld the literacy test ban of the Voting Rights Act of 1965, under Congress' Fifteenth Amendment enforcement power.

As broad as the congressional enforcement power is, it is not unlimited. Specifically, there are at least three limitations upon Congress' power to enforce the guarantees of the Civil War Amendments. First, Congress may not by legislation repeal other provisions of the Constitution. Second, the power granted to Congress was not intended to strip the States of their power to govern themselves or to convert our national government of enumerated powers into a central government of unrestrained authority over every inch of the whole Nation. Third, Congress may only "enforce" the provisions of the amendments, and may do so only by "appropriate legislation." Congress has no power under the enforcement sections to undercut the amendments' guarantees of personal equality and freedom from discrimination, or to undermine those protections of the Bill of Rights which we have held the Fourteenth Amendment made applicable to the States.

Of course, we have upheld congressional legislation under the Enforcement Clauses in some cases where Congress has interfered with state regulation of the local electoral process. In *Katzenbach v. Morgan*, the Court upheld a statute which outlawed New York's requirement of literacy in English as a prerequisite to voting as this requirement was applied to Puerto Ricans with certain educational qualifications. The New York statute overridden by Congress applied to all elections. And in *South Carolina v. Katzenbach*, the Court upheld the literacy test ban of the Voting Rights Act of 1965. That Act proscribed the use of the literacy test in all elections in certain areas. But division of power between state and national governments, like every provision of the Constitution, was expressly qualified by the Civil War Amendments' ban on racial discrimination. Where Congress attempts to remedy racial discrimination under its enforcement powers, its authority is enhanced by the avowed intention of the framers of the Thirteenth, Fourteenth, and Fifteenth Amendments.

Nothing to Do with Race

In enacting the 18-year-old vote provisions of the Act now before the Court, Congress made no legislative findings that the 21-year-old vote requirement was used by the States to disenfranchise voters on account of race. I seriously doubt that such a finding, if made, could be supported by substantial evidence. Since Congress has attempted to invade an area preserved to the States by the Constitution without a foundation for enforcing the Civil War Amendments' ban on racial discrimination, I would hold that Congress has exceeded its powers in attempting to lower the voting age in state and local elections. On the other hand, where Congress legislates in a domain not exclusively reserved by the Constitution to the

States, its enforcement power need not be tied so closely to the goal of eliminating discrimination on account of race.

To invalidate part of the Voting Rights Act Amendments of 1970, however, does not mean that the entire Act must fall, or that the constitutional part of the 18-year-old vote provision cannot be given effect. In passing the Voting Rights Act Amendments of 1970, Congress recognized that the limits of its power under the Enforcement Clauses were largely undetermined, and therefore included a broad severability provision: "If any provision of this Act or the application of any provision thereof to any person or circumstance is judicially determined to be invalid, the remainder of this Act or the application of such provision to other persons or circumstances shall not be affected by such determination."

In this case, it is the judgment of the Court that Title III, lowering the voting age to 18, is invalid as applied to voters in state and local elections. It is also the judgment of the Court that Title III is valid with respect to national elections. We would fail to follow the express will of Congress in interpreting its own statute if we refused to sever these two distinct aspects of Title III. Moreover, it is a longstanding canon of statutory construction that legislative enactments are to be enforced to the extent that they are not inconsistent with the Constitution, particularly where the valid portion of the statute does not depend upon the invalid part. Here, of course, the enforcement of the 18-year-old vote in national elections is in no way dependent upon its enforcement in state and local elections.

Congress Can Set a Minimum Voting Age Under the Equal Protection Clause

William O. Douglas

William O. Douglas was the longest-serving justice in the history of the Supreme Court, of which he was a member from 1939 to 1975. Nicknamed the Lone Ranger because his was often the only dissenting vote in a case, he was a strong supporter of First Amendment rights and of environmental protection. In the following dissent, he argues that the lowering of the voting age by Congress is valid for both federal and state elections under the Equal Protection Clause of the Fourteenth Amendment. The case is no different from many other cases in which the Court has overruled state laws that restricted voting rights, he says; the right to vote is a fundamental civil right that is protected under the Fourteenth Amendment. Although that amendment was originally intended to protect the rights of blacks, in Douglas's opinion the powers it gives to Congress are not limited to situations involving race. It was reasonable, he believed, for Congress to decide that eighteen-year-olds are mature enough to vote and should be allowed to do so. Therefore, he believes that the Voting Rights Act should be upheld.

The grant of the franchise to 18-year-olds by Congress is, in my view, valid across the board.

I suppose that, in 1920, when the Nineteenth Amendment was ratified giving women the right to vote, it was assumed by most constitutional experts that there was no relief by way of the Equal Protection Clause of the Fourteenth Amendment. In *Minor v. Happersett*, the Court held in the 1874 Term that a

William O. Douglas, dissenting opinion, *Oregon v. Mitchell*, U.S. Supreme Court, December 21, 1970.

State could constitutionally restrict the franchise to men. While the Fourteenth Amendment was relied upon, the thrust of the opinion was directed at the Privileges and Immunities Clause with a subsidiary reference to the Due Process Clause. It was much later, indeed not until the 1961 Term—nearly a century after the Fourteenth Amendment was adopted—that discrimination against voters on grounds *other than race* was struck down.

The first case in which this Court struck down a statute under the Equal Protection Clause of the Fourteenth Amendment was *Strauder v. West Virginia*, decided in the 1879 Term. In the 1961 Term, we squarely held that the manner of apportionment of members of a state legislature raised a justiciable question under the Equal Protection Clause, *Baker v. Carr*. That case was followed by numerous others, *e.g.*: that one person could not be given twice or 10 times the voting power of another person in a state-wide election merely because he lived in a rural area or in the smallest rural county; that the principle of equality applied to both Houses of a bicameral legislature; that political parties receive protection under the Equal Protection Clause just as voters do.

The reapportionment cases, however, are not quite in point here, though they are the target of my Brother [Justice John Marshall] Harlan's dissent. His painstaking review of the history of the Equal Protection Clause leads him to conclude that "political" rights are not protected, though "civil" rights are protected. The problem of what questions are "political" has been a recurring issue in this Court from the beginning, and we recently reviewed them all in *Baker v. Carr*, and in *Powell v. McCormack*. *Baker v. Carr* was a reapportionment case, and *Powell v. McCormack* involved the exclusion from the House of Representatives of a Congressman. The issue of "political" question versus "justiciable" question was argued *pro* and *con* in those cases, and my Brother Harlan stated in *Baker v. Carr*, and on related occasions, his views on the con-

Karen Rogers, a nineteen-year-old woman from Chicago, votes in the 1972 Illinois presidential primary. 1972 was the first year that eighteen-year-olds could vote, after passage of the Twenty-sixth Amendment to the Constitution. © Bettmann/Corbis.

stitutional dimensions of the "political" question in the setting of the reapportionment problem.

Those cases involved the question whether legislatures must be so structured as to reflect with approximate equality the voice of every voter. The ultimate question was whether, absent a proper apportionment by the legislature, a federal court could itself make an apportionment. That kind of problem raised issues irrelevant here. Reapportionment, as our experience shows, presented a tangle of partisan politics in which geography, economics, urban life, rural constituencies, and numerous other nonlegal factors play varying roles. The competency of courts to deal with them was challenged. Yet we held the issues were justiciable. None of those so-called "political" questions are involved here.

Right to Vote Must Be Protected

This case, so far as equal protection is concerned, is no whit different from a controversy over a state law that disqualifies women from certain types of employment, or that imposes a heavier punishment on one class of offender than on another whose crime is not intrinsically different. The right to vote is, of course, different in one respect from the other rights in the economic, social, or political field, which are under the Equal Protection Clause. The right to vote is a civil right deeply embedded in the Constitution. Article I, Section 2, provides that the House is composed of members "chosen ... by the People" and the electors "shall have the Qualifications requisite for Electors of the most numerous Branch of the State Legislature." The Seventeenth Amendment states that Senators shall be "elected by the people." The Fifteenth Amendment speaks of the "right of citizens of the United States to vote"—not only in federal but in state elections. The Court in *Ex parte Yarbrough*, stated:

> This new constitutional right was mainly designed for citizens of African descent. The principle, however, that the protection of the exercise of this right is within the power of Congress, is as necessary to the right of other citizens to vote as to the colored citizen, and to the right to vote in general as to the right to be protected against discrimination.

It was in that tradition that we said in *Reynolds v. Sims*, "The right to vote freely for the candidate of one's choice is of the essence of a democratic society, and any restrictions on that right strike at the heart of representative government."

This "right to choose, secured by the Constitution," *United States v. Classic*, is a civil right of the highest order. Voting concerns "political" matters; but the right is not "political" in the constitutional sense. Interference with it has given rise to a long and consistent line of decisions by the Court; and the claim has always been upheld as justiciable. Whatever distinction may have been made, following the Civil War, between "civil" and "political" rights, has passed into history. In *Harper v. Virginia Board of Elections*, we stated: "Notions of what constitutes equal treatment for purposes of the Equal Protection Clause do change." That statement is in harmony with my view of the Fourteenth Amendment, as expressed by my Brother [Justice William] Brennan: "We must therefore conclude that its framers understood their Amendment to be a broadly worded injunction capable of being interpreted by future generations in accordance with the vision and needs of those generations."

Hence, the history of the Fourteenth Amendment tendered by my Brother Harlan is irrelevant to the present problem.

Since the right is civil and not "political," it is protected by the Equal Protection Clause of the Fourteenth Amendment which in turn, by Section 5 of that Amendment, can be "enforced" by Congress.

Other Pertinent Cases

In *Carrington v. Rash*, we held that Texas could not bar a person, otherwise qualified, from voting merely because he was a member of the armed services. Occupation, we held, when used to bar a person from voting, was that invidious discrimination which the Equal Protection Clause condemns. In *Evans v. Cornman*, we held that a State could not deny the vote to residents of a federal enclave when it treated them as residents for many other purposes. In *Harper v. Virginia Board of Elections*, we held a State could not in harmony with the Equal Protection Clause keep a person from voting in state elections because of "the affluence of the voter or payment of any fee." In *Kramer v. Union School District*, we held that a person could not be barred from voting in school board elections merely because he was a bachelor. So far as the Equal Protection Clause was concerned, we said that the line between those qualified to vote and those not qualified turns on whether those excluded have "a distinct and direct interest in the school meeting decisions." In *Cipriano v. City of Houma*, we held that a state law which gave only "property taxpayers" the right to vote on the issuance of revenue bonds of a municipal utility system violated equal protection as "the benefits and burdens of the bond issue fall indiscriminately on property owner and nonproperty owner alike." And only on June 23, 1970, we held in *Phoenix v. Kolodziejski*, that it violates equal protection to restrict those who may vote on general obligation bonds to real property taxpayers. We looked to see if there was any "compelling state interest" in the voting restrictions. We held that "nonproperty owners" are not "substantially less interested in the issuance of these securities than are property owners," and that, presumptively, "when all citizens are affected in important ways by a governmental decision subject to a referendum, the Constitution does not permit weighted voting or the exclusion of otherwise qualified citizens from the franchise."

And as recently as November 9, 1970, we summarily affirmed a district court decision on the basis of *Kolodziejski*: *Parish School Board of St. Charles v. Stewart*, where Louisiana gave a vote on municipal bond issues only to "property taxpayers."

The powers granted Congress by Section 5 of the Fourteenth Amendment to "enforce" the Equal Protection Clause are "the same broad powers expressed in the Necessary and Proper Clause, Art. I, Sec. 8." *Katzenbach v. Morgan.* As we stated in that case, "Correctly viewed, Section 5 is a positive grant of legislative power authorizing Congress to exercise its discretion in determining whether and what legislation is needed to secure the guarantees of the Fourteenth Amendment."

Reduction in Voting Age Needed

Congress might well conclude that a reduction in the voting age from 21 to 18 was needed in the interest of equal protection. The Act itself brands the denial of the franchise to 18-

year-olds as "a particularly unfair treatment of such citizens in view of the national defense responsibilities imposed" on them. The fact that only males are drafted while the vote extends to females as well is not relevant, for the female component of these families or prospective families is also caught up in war, and hit hard by it. Congress might well believe that men and women alike should share the fateful decision.

It is said, why draw the line at 18? Why not 17? Congress can draw lines, and I see no reason why it cannot conclude that 18-year-olds have that degree of maturity which entitles them to the franchise. They are generally considered by American law to be mature enough to contract, to marry, to drive an automobile, to own a gun, and to be responsible for criminal behavior as an adult.

Moreover, we are advised that, under state laws, mandatory school attendance does not, as a matter of practice, extend beyond the age of 18. On any of these items, the States, of course, have leeway to raise or lower the age requirements. But voting is "a fundamental matter in a free and democratic society," *Reynolds v. Sims.* Where "fundamental rights and liberties are asserted under the Equal Protection Clause, classifications which might invade or restrain them must be closely scrutinized and carefully confined." *Harper v. Virginia Board of Elections.* There, we were speaking of state restrictions on those rights. Here, we are dealing with the right of Congress to "enforce" the principles of equality enshrined in the Fourteenth Amendment. The right to "enforce" granted by Section 5 of that Amendment is, as noted, parallel with the Necessary and Proper Clause, whose reach Chief Justice Marshall described in *McCulloch v. Maryland*: "Let the end be legitimate, let it be within the scope of the constitution, and all means which are appropriate, which are plainly adapted to that end, which are not prohibited, but consist with the letter and spirit of the constitution, are constitutional."

Equality of voting by all who are deemed mature enough to vote is certainly consistent "with the letter and spirit of the constitution." Much is made of the fact that Art. I, Sec. 4, of the Constitution gave Congress only the power to regulate the "Manner of holding Elections," not the power to fix qualifications for voting in elections. But the Civil War Amendments—the Thirteenth, Fourteenth, and Fifteenth—made vast inroads on the power of the States. Equal protection became a standard for state action and Congress was given authority to "enforce" it. The manner of enforcement involves discretion; but that discretion is largely entrusted to the Congress, not to the courts. If racial discrimination were the only concern of the Equal Protection Clause, then across-the-board voting regulations set by the States would be of no concern to Congress. But it is much too late in history to make that claim. Moreover, election inequalities created by state laws and based on factors other than race may violate the Equal Protection Clause, as we have held over and over again. The reach of Section 5 to "enforce" equal protection by eliminating election inequalities would seem quite broad. Certainly there is not a word of limitation in Section 5 which would restrict its applicability to matters of race alone. And if, as stated in *McCulloch v. Maryland*, the measure of the power of Congress is whether the remedy is consistent "with the letter and spirit of the constitution," we should have no difficulty here. We said in *Gray v. Sanders*: "The conception of political equality from the Declaration of Independence, to Lincoln's Gettysburg Address, to the Fifteenth, Seventeenth, and Nineteenth Amendments can mean only one thing—one person, one vote."

It is a reasoned judgment that those who have such a large "stake" in modern elections as 18-year-olds, whether, in times of war or peace, should have political equality. As was made plain in the dissent in *Colegrove v. Green*, the Equal Protection Clause does service to protect the right to vote in federal as well as in state elections.

I would sustain the choice which Congress has made.

Congress Is Not Authorized to Set a Minimum Voting Age

John Marshall Harlan

John Marshall Harlan was a justice of the Supreme Court from 1955 to 1971. (His grandfather, who had the same name, served on the Court earlier.) He is regarded as one of the twentieth century's most influential justices. He was conservative in his interpretation of the Constitution and did not believe that the Fourteenth Amendment made the Bill of Rights applicable to state laws. In the following dissenting opinion he argues that the history of the Fourteenth Amendment indicates that it was not intended to restrict the power of the states to allocate political power by setting qualifications for voting in either federal or state elections. Whether eighteen-year-olds are mature enough to vote is not the issue, he argues; it is a matter on which reasonable people may differ and which the Constitution gives the states, not Congress, the power to decide. The suggestion that eighteen-year-olds are threatened with unconstitutional discrimination is in his view "fanciful." He therefore maintains that in attempting to lower the voting age, Congress exceeded its authority.

I am of the opinion that the Fourteenth Amendment was never intended to restrict the authority of the States to allocate their political power as they see fit, and therefore that it does not authorize Congress to set voter qualifications, in either state or federal elections. I find no other source of congressional power to lower the voting age as fixed by state laws. . . .

It is fitting to begin with a quotation from one of the leading members of the 39th Congress, which proposed the

John Marshall Harlan, dissenting opinion, *Oregon v. Mitchell*, U.S. Supreme Court, December 21, 1970.

Fourteenth Amendment to the States in 1866: "Every Constitution embodies the principles of its framers. It is a transcript of their minds. If its meaning in any place is open to doubt, or if words are used which seem to have no fixed signification, we cannot err if we turn to the framers; and their authority increases in proportion to the evidence which they have left on the question." (Sen. [Charles] Sumner)

Believing this view to be undoubtedly sound, I turn to the circumstances in which the Fourteenth Amendment was adopted for enlightenment on the intended reach of its provisions. This, for me, necessary undertaking has unavoidably led to an opinion of more than ordinary length. Except for those who are willing to close their eyes to constitutional history in making constitutional interpretations or who read such history with a preconceived determination to attain a particular constitutional goal, I think that the history of the Fourteenth Amendment makes it clear beyond any reasonable doubt that no part of the legislation now under review can be upheld as a legitimate exercise of congressional power under that Amendment. . . .

No one asserts that the power to set voting qualifications was taken from the States or subjected to federal control by any Amendment before the Fourteenth. The historical evidence makes it plain that the Congress and the States proposing and ratifying that Amendment affirmatively understood that they were not limiting state power over voting qualifications. The existence of the power therefore survived the amending process, and, except as it has been limited by the Fifteenth, Nineteenth, and Twenty-fourth Amendments, it still exists today. Indeed, the very fact that constitutional amendments were deemed necessary to bring about federal abolition of state restrictions on voting by reason of race (Amdt. XV), sex (Amdt. XIX), and, even with respect to federal elections, the failure to pay state poll taxes (Amdt. XXIV), is itself forceful evidence of the common understanding in 1869, 1919, and

1962, respectively, that the Fourteenth Amendment did not empower Congress to legislate in these respects. . . .

As the Court is not justified in substituting its own views of wise policy for the commands of the Constitution, still less is it justified in allowing Congress to disregard those commands as the Court understands them. . . .

A Matter for State Judgment

Even on the assumption that the Fourteenth Amendment does place a limit on the sorts of voter qualifications which a State may adopt, I still do not see any real force in the reasoning.

When my Brothers refer to "complex factual questions," they call to mind disputes about primary, objective facts dealing with such issues as the number of persons between the ages of 18 and 21, the extent of their education, and so forth. The briefs of the four States in these cases take no issue with respect to any of the facts of this nature presented to Congress and relied on by my Brothers. Except for one or two matters of dubious relevance, these facts are not subject to rational dispute. The disagreement in these cases revolves around the evaluation of this largely uncontested factual material. On the assumption that maturity and experience are relevant to intelligent and responsible exercise of the elective franchise, are the immaturity and inexperience of the average 18-, 19-, or 20-year-old sufficiently serious to justify denying such a person a direct voice in decisions affecting his or her life? Whether or not this judgment is characterized as "factual," it calls for striking a balance between incommensurate interests. Where the balance is to be struck depends ultimately on the values and the perspective of the decisionmaker. It is a matter as to which men of good will can and do reasonably differ.

I fully agree that judgments of the sort involved here are beyond the institutional competence and constitutional authority of the judiciary. They are preeminently matters for legislative discretion, with judicial review, if it exists at all, narrowly limited. But the same reasons which, in my view, would require the judiciary to sustain a reasonable state resolution of the issue also require Congress to abstain from entering the picture.

Judicial deference is based not on relative factfinding competence, but on due regard for the decision of the body constitutionally appointed to decide. Establishment of voting qualifications is a matter for state legislatures. Assuming any authority at all, only when the Court can say with some confidence that the legislature has demonstrably erred in adjusting the competing interests is it justified in striking down the legislative judgment. This order of things is more efficient and more congenial to our system, and, in my judgment, much more likely to achieve satisfactory results than one in which the Court has a free hand to replace state legislative judgments with its own.

The same considerations apply, and with almost equal force, to Congress' displacement of state decisions with its own ideas of wise policy. The sole distinction between Congress and the Court in this regard is that Congress, being an elective body, presumptively has popular authority for the value judgment it makes. But since the state legislature has a like authority, this distinction between Congress and the judiciary falls short of justifying a congressional veto on the state judgment. The perspectives and values of national legislators on the issue of voting qualifications are likely to differ from those of state legislators, but I see no reason *a priori* [deductively] to prefer those of the national figures, whose collective decision, applying nationwide, is necessarily less able to take account of peculiar local conditions. Whether one agrees with this judgment or not, it is the one expressed by the Framers in leaving voter qualifications to the States. . . .

Sources of Congressional Power

Since I cannot agree that the Fourteenth Amendment empowered Congress, or the federal judiciary, to control voter qualifications, I turn to other asserted sources of congressional power. My Brother [Justice Hugo] Black would find that such power exists with respect to *federal* elections by virtue of Art. I, Sec. 4, and seemingly other considerations that he finds implicit in federal authority.

The constitutional provisions controlling the regulation of congressional elections are the following: Art. I, Sec. 2: "The Electors [for representatives] in each State shall have the Qualifications requisite for Electors of the most numerous Branch of the State Legislature."

Art. I, Sec. 4: "The Times, Places and Manner of holding Elections for Senators and Representatives, shall be prescribed in each State by the Legislature thereof; but the Congress may at any time by Law make or alter such Regulations, except as to the Places of chusing Senators."

Amdt. XVII: "The electors [for senators] in each State shall have the qualifications requisite for electors of the most numerous branch of the State legislatures."

It is difficult to see how words could be clearer in stating what Congress can control and what it cannot control. Surely nothing in these provisions lends itself to the view that voting qualifications in federal elections are to be set by Congress. The reason for the scheme is not hard to find. In the Constitutional Convention [James] Madison expressed the view that: "The qualifications of electors and elected were fundamental articles in a Republican Govt. and ought to be fixed by the Constitution. If the Legislature could regulate those of either, it can by degrees subvert the Constitution." . . .

As to presidential elections, the Constitution provides: "Each State shall appoint, in such Manner as the Legislature thereof may direct, a Number of Electors. . . ." Art. II, Sec. 1, "The Congress may determine the Time of chusing the Electors, and the Day on which they shall give their Votes; which Day shall be the same throughout the United States." Art. II, Sec. 1.

Even the power to control the "Manner" of holding elections, given with respect to congressional elections by Art. I, Sec. 4, is absent with respect to the selection of presidential electors. And, of course, the fact that it was deemed necessary to provide separately for congressional power to regulate the time of choosing presidential electors and the President himself demonstrates that the power over "Times, Places and Manner" given by Art. I, Sec. 4, does not refer to presidential elections, but only to the elections for Congressmen. Any shadow of a justification for congressional power with respect to congressional elections therefore disappears utterly in presidential elections. . . .

No Threat of Discrimination

The only constitutional basis advanced in support of the lowering of the voting age is the power to enforce the Equal Protection Clause, a power found in Section 5 of the Fourteenth Amendment. For the reasons already given, it cannot be said that the statutory provision is valid as declaratory of the meaning of that clause. Its validity therefore must rest on congressional power to lower the voting age as a means of preventing invidious discrimination that is within the purview of that clause.

The history of the Fourteenth Amendment may well foreclose the possibility that Section 5 empowers Congress to enfranchise a class of citizens so that they may protect themselves against discrimination forbidden by the first section, but it is unnecessary for me to explore that question. For I think it fair to say that the suggestion that members of the age group between 18 and 21 are threatened with unconstitutional discrimination, or that any hypothetical discrimination is likely to be affected by lowering the voting age, is little short of fanciful. I see no justification for stretching to find any such possibility when all the evidence indicates that Congress—led on by recent decisions of this Court—thought simply that 18-year-olds were fairly entitled to the vote and that Congress could give it to them by legislation.

I therefore conclude, for these and other reasons given in this opinion, that, in Section 302 of the Voting Rights Act Amendments of 1970, Congress exceeded its delegated powers.

No Legitimate Reason Exists for States Not to Allow Voting at Age Eighteen

William J. Brennan

William J. Brennan was a justice of the Supreme Court from 1956 to 1990. He was a strong liberal who was influential in expanding the Court's view of individual rights. In the following dissenting opinion he argues that granting the vote to citizens over twenty-one while denying it to those between eighteen and and twenty-one is a violation of the Fourteenth Amendment's Equal Protection Clause. All the states treat citizens eighteen and older the same as others as far as criminal prosecution is concerned. Also, the fact that they may be less educated than their elders is irrelevant because people over twenty-one have the right to vote even if they never finished school. Nothing has been said, Brennan argues, that suggests eighteen-year-olds in states where they are allowed to vote are not as responsible as older people, and the young people in other states cannot be reasonably considered less mature. Thus states do not have any legitimate reason to say that excluding them from the franchise is necessary to assure intelligent and responsible voting, and so doing is, in Brennan's opinion, clearly unconstitutional.

The final question presented by these cases is the propriety of Title III of the 1970 Amendments, which forbids the States from disenfranchising persons over the age of 18 because of their age. Congress was of the view that this prohibition, embodied in Section 302 of the Amendments, was necessary among other reasons in order to enforce the Equal Protection Clause of the Fourteenth Amendment. The States involved in the present litigation question the assertion of congressional power to make that judgment.

William J. Brennan, dissenting opinion, *Oregon v. Mitchell*, U.S. Supreme Court, December 21, 1970.

It is important at the outset to recognize what is not involved in these cases. We are not faced with an assertion of congressional power to regulate any and all aspects of state and federal elections, or even to make general rules for the determination of voter qualifications. Nor are we faced with the assertion that Congress is possessed of plenary [full] power to set minimum ages for voting throughout the States. Every State in the Union has conceded by statute that citizens 21 years of age and over are capable of intelligent and responsible exercise of the right to vote. The single, narrow question presented by these cases is whether Congress was empowered to conclude, as it did, that citizens 18 to 21 years of age are not substantially less able.

We believe there is serious question whether a statute granting the franchise to citizens 21 and over while denying it to those between the ages of 18 and 21 could, in any event, withstand present scrutiny under the Equal Protection Clause. Regardless of the answer to this question, however, it is clear to us that proper regard for the special function of Congress in making determinations of legislative fact compels this Court to respect those determinations unless they are contradicted by evidence far stronger than anything that has been adduced [used as example] in these cases. We would uphold Section 302 as a valid exercise of congressional power under Section 5 of the Fourteenth Amendment.

All parties to these cases are agreed that the States are given power, under the Constitution, to determine the qualifications for voting in state elections. But it is now settled that exercise of this power, like all other exercises of state power, is subject to the Equal Protection Clause of the Fourteenth Amendment. Although it once was thought that equal protection required only that a given legislative classification, once made, be evenly applied, for more than 70 years we have consistently held that the classifications embodied in a state statute must also meet the requirements of equal protection.

Right to Vote Is Fundamental

The right to vote has long been recognized as a "fundamental political right, because [it is] preservative of all rights."

Consequently, when exclusions from the franchise are challenged as violating the Equal Protection Clause, judicial scrutiny is not confined to the question whether the exclusion may reasonably be thought to further a permissible interest of the State. "A more exacting standard obtains." In such cases, "the Court must determine whether the exclusions are necessary to promote a compelling state interest."

In the present cases, the States justify exclusion of 18- to 21-year-olds from the voting rolls solely on the basis of the States' interests in promoting intelligent and responsible exercise of the franchise. There is no reason to question the legitimacy and importance of these interests. But standards of intelligence and responsibility, however defined, may permissibly be applied only to the means whereby a prospective voter determines how to exercise his choice, and not to the actual choice itself. Were it otherwise, such standards could all too easily serve as mere epithets designed to cloak the exclusion of a class of voters simply because of the way they might vote. Such a state purpose is, of course, constitutionally impermissible. We must, therefore, examine with particular care the asserted connection between age limitations and the admittedly laudable state purpose to further intelligent and responsible voting.

We do not lack a starting point for this inquiry. Although the question has never been squarely presented, we have in the past indicated that age is a factor not necessarily irrelevant to qualifications for voting. But recognition that age is not in all circumstances a "capricious or irrelevant factor," *Harper v. Virginia Board of Elections*, does not insure the validity of the particular limitation involved here. Every State in the Union has concluded for itself that citizens 21 years of age and over are capable of responsible and intelligent voting. Accepting this judgment, there remains the question whether citizens 18 to 21 years of age may fairly be said to be less able.

State practice itself in other areas casts doubt upon any such proposition. Each of the 50 States has provided special mechanisms for dealing with persons who are deemed insufficiently mature and intelligent to understand, and to conform their behavior to, the criminal laws of the State. Forty-nine of the States have concluded that, in this regard, 18-year-olds are invariably to be dealt with according to precisely the same standards prescribed for their elders. This at the very least is evidence of a nearly unanimous legislative judgment on the part of the States themselves that differences in maturity and intelligence between 18-year-olds and persons 21 years of age and over are too trivial to warrant specialized treatment for any of the former class in the critically important matter of criminal responsibility. Similarly, every State permits 18-year-olds to marry, and 39 States do not require parental consent for such persons of one or both sexes. State statutory practice in other areas follows along these lines, albeit not as consistently.

Not Dependent on Education

Uniform state practice in the field of education points the same way. No State in the Union requires attendance at school beyond the age of 18. Of course, many 18-year-olds continue their education to 21 and beyond. But no 18-year-old who does not do so will be disenfranchised thereby once he reaches the age of 21. Whether or not a State could in any circumstances condition exercise of the franchise upon educational achievements beyond the level reached by 18-year-olds today, there is no question but that no State purports to do so. Accordingly, that 18-year-olds as a class may be less educated than some of their elders cannot justify restriction of the franchise, for the States themselves have determined that this in-

First in line, Sally Comerford, eighteen, registers at the Chicago Board of Elections Commissioners in Chicago's City Hall on August 3, 1970. She was first during the first day of voter registration for persons between the ages of eighteen and twenty-one. © Bettmann/Corbis.

cremental education is irrelevant to voting qualifications. And finally, we have been cited to no material whatsoever that would support the proposition that intelligence, as opposed to educational attainment, increases between the ages of 18 and 21.

One final point remains. No State seeking to uphold its denial of the franchise to 18-year-olds has adduced anything beyond the mere difference in age. We have already indicated that the relevance of this difference is contradicted by nearly uniform state practice in other areas. But perhaps more important is the uniform experience of those States—Georgia since 1943, and Kentucky since 1955—that have permitted 18-year-olds to vote. We have not been directed to a word of testimony or other evidence that would indicate either that 18-year-olds in those States have voted any less intelligently and responsibly than their elders, or that there is any reasonable ground for belief that 18-year-olds in other States are less able than those in Georgia and Kentucky. On the other hand, every person who spoke to the issue in either the House or Senate was agreed that 18-year-olds in both States were at least as interested, able, and responsible in voting as were their elders.

In short, we are faced with an admitted restriction upon the franchise, supported only by bare assertions and long practice, in the face of strong indications that the States themselves do not credit the factual propositions upon which the restriction is asserted to rest. But there is no reason for us to decide whether, in a proper case, we would be compelled to hold this restriction a violation of the Equal Protection Clause. For, as our decisions have long made clear, the question we face today is not one of judicial power under the Equal Protection Clause. The question is the scope of congressional power under Section 5 of the Fourteenth Amendment. . . .

The historical record left by the framers of the Fourteenth Amendment, because it is a product of differing and conflicting political pressures and conceptions of federalism, is thus too vague and imprecise to provide us with sure guidance in deciding the pending cases. We must therefore conclude that its framers understood their Amendment to be a broadly worded injunction capable of being interpreted by future generations in accordance with the vision and needs of those generations. We would be remiss in our duty if, in an attempt to find certainty amidst uncertainty, we were to misread the historical record and cease to interpret the Amendment as this Court has always interpreted it.

No Legitimate Purpose

There remains only the question whether Congress could rationally have concluded that denial of the franchise to citizens between the ages of 18 and 21 was unnecessary to promote any legitimate interests of the States in assuring intelligent and responsible voting. There is no need to set out the legislative history of Title III at any great length here. Proposals to lower the voting age to 18 had been before Congress at several times since 1942. The Senate Subcommittee on Constitutional Amendments conducted extensive hearings on the matter in 1968 and again in 1970, and the question was discussed at some length on the floor of both the House and the Senate.

Congress was aware, of course, of the facts and state practices already discussed. It was aware of the opinion of many historians that choice of the age of 21 as the age of maturity was an outgrowth of medieval requirements of time for military training and development of a physique adequate to bear heavy armor. It knew that, whereas only six percent of 18-year-olds in 1900 had completed high school, 81 percent have done so today. Congress was aware that 18-year-olds today make up a not insubstantial proportion of the adult workforce; and it was entitled to draw upon its experience in supervising the federal establishment to determine the competence and responsibility with which 18-year-olds perform their assigned tasks. As Congress recognized, its judgment that 18-year-olds are capable of voting is consistent with its practice of entrusting them with the heavy responsibilities of military service. Finally, Congress was presented with evidence that the age of social and biological maturity in modern society has been consistently decreasing. Dr. Margaret Mead, an anthropologist, testified that, in the past century, the "age of physical maturity has been dropping and has dropped over 3 years." Many Senators and Representatives, including several involved in national campaigns, testified from personal experience that 18-year-olds of today appeared at least as mature and intelligent as 21-year-olds in the Congressmen's youth.

Finally, and perhaps most important, Congress had before it information on the experience of two States, Georgia and Kentucky, which have allowed 18-year-olds to vote since 1943 and 1955, respectively. Every elected Representative from those States who spoke to the issue agreed that, as Senator [Herman] Talmadge stated, "young people [in these States] have made the sophisticated decisions and have assumed the mature responsibilities of voting. Their performance has exceeded the greatest hopes and expectations."

In sum, Congress had ample evidence upon which it could have based the conclusion that exclusion of citizens 18 to 21 years of age from the franchise is wholly unnecessary to promote any legitimate interest the States may have in assuring intelligent and responsible voting. If discrimination is unnecessary to promote any legitimate state interest, it is plainly unconstitutional under the Equal Protection Clause, and Congress has ample power to forbid it under Section 5 of the Fourteenth Amendment. We would uphold Section 302 of the 1970 Amendments as a legitimate exercise of congressional power.

Only a Constitutional Amendment Can Override the States' Right to Set Their Voting Ages

Potter Stewart

Potter Stewart was a justice of the Supreme Court from 1958 to 1981. He was a moderate who believed that the Court often interpreted the meaning of constitutional amendments in ways their framers did not intend. In the following dissent he argues that the Court is not being asked whether a lower voting age is a good idea, but only whether Congress has the authority to lower it. He maintains that it does not. Constitutional amendments were needed to grant voting rights to blacks and to women, yet it is claimed that if Congress concludes that laws setting the voting age at twenty-one are not required by a compelling state interest, it can nullify them under the Equal Protection Clause. This cannot be true, he says, because the Constitution gives the states power to establish voter qualifications although they could not demonstrate a compelling interest in choosing one age rather than another. Whereas Congress has passed other laws involving voting rights, these were to eliminate the discrimination against ethnic minorities that was a clear violation of equal protection. In his opinion these past decisions did not give Congress the right to decide which state interests are "compelling."

In these cases, we deal with the constitutional validity of three provisions of the Voting Rights Act Amendments of 1970. Congress undertook in these provisions: (a) to abolish for a five-year period all literacy tests and similar voting eligi-

Potter Stewart, dissenting opinion, *Oregon v. Mitchell*, U.S. Supreme Court, December 21, 1970.

bility requirements imposed by any State in the Union (b) to remove the restrictions imposed by state durational residency requirements upon voters in presidential elections and (c) to reduce the voting age to a minimum of 18 years for all voters in all elections throughout the Nation. The Court today upholds section 201's nationwide literacy test ban and section 202's elimination of state durational residency restrictions in presidential elections. Section 302's extension of the franchise to 18-year-old voters is (by virtue of the opinion of Mr. Justice [Hugo] Black announcing the judgments of the Court) upheld as applied to federal elections.... I disagree with the Court's conclusion that Congress could constitutionally reduce the voting age to 18 for federal elections, since I am convinced that Congress was wholly without constitutional power to alter—for the purpose of any election—the voting age qualifications now determined by the several States.

Before turning to a discussion of my views, it seems appropriate to state that we are not called upon in these cases to evaluate or appraise the wisdom of abolishing literacy tests, of altering state residency requirements, or of reducing the voting age to 18. Whatever we may think as citizens, our single duty as judges is to determine whether the legislation before us was within the constitutional power of Congress to enact. I find it necessary to state so elementary a proposition only because certain of the separate opinions filed today contain many pages devoted to a demonstration of how beneficent are the goals of this legislation, particularly the extension of the electoral franchise to young men and women of 18. A casual reader could easily get the impression that what we are being asked in these cases is whether or not we think allowing people 18 years old to vote is a good idea. Nothing could be wider of the mark. My Brothers to the contrary, there is no question here as to the "judgment" of Congress; there are questions only of Congress' constitutional power....

Congress Cannot Alter Voting Age

Section 302 added by the Voting Rights Act. Amendments of 1970 undertakes to enfranchise in all federal, state, and local elections those citizens 18 years of age or older who are now denied the right to vote by state law because they have not reached the age of 21. Although it was found necessary to amend the Constitution in order to confer a federal right to vote upon Negroes and upon females, the Government asserts that a federal right to vote can be conferred upon people between 18 and 21 years of age simply by this Act of Congress. Our decision in *Katzenbach v. Morgan*, it is said, established the power of Congress, under Section 5 of the Fourteenth Amendment, to nullify state laws requiring voters to be 21 years of age or older if Congress could rationally have concluded that such laws are not supported by a "compelling state interest."

In my view, neither the *Morgan* case, nor any other case upon which the Government relies, establishes such congressional power, even assuming that all those cases were rightly decided. Mr. Justice Black is surely correct when he writes,

> It is a plain fact of history that the Framers never imagined that the national Congress would set the qualifications for voters in every election from President to local constable or village alderman. It is obvious that the whole Constitution reserves to the States the power to set voter qualifications in state and local elections, except to the limited extent that the people through constitutional amendments have specifically narrowed the powers of the States. . . .

It is equally plain to me that the Constitution just as completely withholds from Congress the power to alter by legislation qualifications for voters in federal elections, in view of the explicit provisions of Article I, Article II, and the Seventeenth Amendment.

To be sure, recent decisions have established that state action regulating suffrage is not immune from the impact of the

Equal Protection Clause. But we have been careful in those decisions to note the undoubted power of a State to establish a qualification for voting based on age. Indeed, none of the opinions filed today suggests that the States have anything but a constitutionally unimpeachable interest in establishing some age qualification as such. Yet to test the power to establish an age qualification by the "compelling interest" standard is really to deny a State any choice at all, because no State could demonstrate a "compelling interest" in drawing the line with respect to age at one point, rather than another. Obviously, the power to establish an age qualification must carry with it the power to choose a reasonable voting age, as the vast majority of the States have done.

No Discrimination Involved

Katzenbach v. Morgan, does not hold that Congress has the power to determine what are and what are not "compelling state interests" for equal protection purposes. In *Morgan* the Court considered the power of Congress to enact a statute whose principal effect was to enfranchise Puerto Ricans who had moved to New York after receiving their education in Spanish language Puerto Rican schools and who were denied the right to vote in New York because they were unable to read or write English. The Court upheld the statute on two grounds: that Congress could conclude that enhancing the political power of the Puerto Rican community by conferring the right to vote was an appropriate means of remedying discriminatory treatment in public services, and that Congress could conclude that the New York statute was tainted by the impermissible purpose of denying the right to vote to Puerto Ricans, an undoubted invidious discrimination under the Equal Protection Clause. Both of these decisional grounds were far-reaching. The Court's opinion made clear that Congress could impose on the States a remedy for the denial of equal protection that elaborated upon the direct command of the Constitution, and that it could override state laws on the ground that they were in fact, used as instruments of invidious discrimination even though a court in an individual lawsuit might not have reached that factual conclusion.

But it is necessary to go much further to sustain Section 302. The state laws that it invalidates do not invidiously discriminate against any discrete and insular minority. Unlike the statute considered in *Morgan*, Section 302 is valid only if Congress has the power not only to provide the means of eradicating situations that amount to a violation of the Equal Protection Clause, but also to determine as a matter of substantive constitutional law what situations fall within the ambit [scope] of the clause, and what state interests are "compelling." I concurred in Mr. Justice [John Marshall] Harlan's dissent in *Morgan*. That case, as I now read it, gave congressional power under Section 5 the furthest possible legitimate reach. Yet to sustain the constitutionality of Section 302 would require an enormous extension of that decision's rationale. I cannot but conclude that Section 302 was beyond the constitutional power of Congress to enact.

Amendment XXVI and Its Consequences

Teens Have Mixed Feelings About Gaining the Vote

Mary Lou Loper

Mary Lou Loper was a staff writer for the Los Angeles Times *when she wrote the following article. It was published during the period before the passage of the Twenty-sixth Amendment, when young people between the ages of eighteen and twenty-one could vote in federal but not state or local elections. Her interviews with some of them reveal that their views of the voting privilege differed widely. Some were incensed that they could not vote for governor or mayor. Some who worked full-time felt that if they were old enough to earn a living, they should be considered competent to vote. But there were no major celebrations in high schools when the Supreme Court announced that eighteen-year-olds could vote in national elections. Many were not bothering to register because they would be twenty-one by the time of the next national election. Some young people believed that the responsibility of voting would make teens assume a more mature attitude, but others felt they had not formed their own opinions well enough to vote and would be influenced largely by their parents or friends.*

Now that they can vote for President, 18-year-olds are incensed that they cannot vote for governor and mayor.

Jim Lacy, for one, freshman president at USC [University of Southern California], calls it "piecemeal legislation."

"We are half-legal," he said. "If an 18-year-old can vote for President, he should be able to vote for other officials, buy liquor, conduct his own financial matters legally, buy a car on credit. Make the 18-year-old an entirely legal person or push everything back to 21, including the draft age."

Mary Lou Loper, "How Teens View the Vote Privilege," *Los Angeles Times*, January 28, 1971, p. G1. Copyright © 1971 Los Angeles Times. Reproduced by permission.

Busy Schedule

Lacy, 18 and interested in a law career, is a full-time student Monday through Friday, flies home to Fremont [in the San Francisco Bay Area] on weekends and works in his father's janitorial business.

"In summer I work 40–50 hours a week; I'm not here on scholarship," he said. "The law says an 18-year-old can go out and work 40 hours a week for a minimum wage. If the law says you are old enough to work, and if the government thinks you are competent to earn a living for yourself and not leech off the government and your parents, then you should be competent enough to vote."

A check with local high schools and colleges reveals no major celebrations when the Supreme Court announced that 18-year-olds could vote.

No Big Rush

Nor has a significantly large number of the 18–21-year-old group rushed out to register to vote.

James S. Allison, county registrar-recorder, said that only 7,049 persons under 21 had registered.

But, he pointed out, a lot of 19- and 20-year-olds will be 21 when the next national election rolls around (June, 1972) so they are not bothering to register now, anyway. This includes his own son, Stewart Allison, 19.

In November elections, Allison said that only 2,386,000 of the 3,116,000 registered voters bothered to go to the polls: thus, some 730,000 automatically canceled their registrations.

Will the 18–19–20 group be any more enthusiastic about voting rights?

Barkley Simpson, 18-year-old Occidental College psychology major, thinks so. He thinks interested 18-year-olds will encourage their peers.

Malou Parent (back to camera), a government teacher, talks with student Charles Barbosa during class in 2004. "The [Iraq] war situation has definitely opened the eyes of a lot of youth," said Barbosa, an eighteen-year-old senior who voted for the first time in the 2004 presidential election. AP Images.

"People of older ages have emotional outlets such as jobs and children," he said. "But young people are excited about wanting to change the country and make it a better place. This is their emotional outlet."

Seen as a Chance

From a ghetto in Cleveland, Simpson views the vote "as a chance to participate rather than demonstrate."

David Feitler, 18-year-old UCLA [University of California, Los Angeles] chemistry major, Wayne Willcox, 18, Polytechnic School (Pasadena) senior, and Daniel Rudolph, 21, Caltech math major, all believe that the responsibility of voting will breed higher responsibility among the new voters.

"You are given more responsibility; you accept more responsibility," said Feitler.

Said Willcox, "As voters, 18-year-olds will have to assume a more mature attitude toward our society. As long as they have the right to vote, they therefore will have to accept the responsibility of accepting what the majority believes."

"I believe that at 18, a person really has his moral standards and basic beliefs and that most 18-year-olds are capable of good judgment. We also are a generation accustomed to change, and being accustomed to this, the level of maturity continues to rise, and we cope with things faster."

Said Rudolph, "I don't think I am any more mature now than I was three years ago at 18; perhaps more experienced, but the experience I have gained is because I have been given more responsibility, and if I had been given that responsibility earlier, I would be that much more responsible."

Will parents influence them?

Opinions vary, but Nancy Woolf, 18-year-old UCLA art history major, admitted: "The first thing I will do is talk to my father and I am sure that is what most 18-year-olds will do. I think more boys will vote on their own, but I think most girls will be influenced by their parents."

"Something makes me think that the majority of 18-year-olds are not mature enough to vote seriously and look at the pros and cons of issues. I think they will tend to vote on what their friends say, on general rumor, such as reading one newspaper, picking up an opinion and letting it go at that."

"For myself, I'm glad I have the vote. It's a responsibility, not a chore, and an honor, but it's time-consuming and it will take some work."

Forming Opinions

Debbie Dillard, 19, USC freshman in liberal arts, said she opposes the 18-year-old vote: "I feel we are still forming opinions, that we are caught up in our schools and jobs and figuring out what we are going to be."

Marlborough high school senior, Cindy James, 18, believes however, that the change is good: "One reason is that youth today, unlike other generations, is more conducive to open expression of social consciousness."

"Past generations may have had ideas on how the government should be run, but the atmosphere was not as urgent as it is now, for instance, with the problems of pollution concerning everyone in a personal way. I'm not saying that all youth will be open to this: a lot will be apathetic, but I think there will be a lot of open expression, and the fact that I can vote will urge me to examine political problems more closely because I will be able to take action on them by voting."

"I think adults look on this generation as being irresponsible, because they have given us everything. They have made it easy for us to do everything, but the fact that we will be allowed to vote will create a sense of responsibility, because responsibility comes with the chance to act responsibly."

Said Sharon Maloney, 18, a Pasadena City College freshman, "If an 18-year-old isn't qualified to vote, then it's his own fault."

Vested Prestige

Feitler at UCLA predicts that in this country adults believe "there is a vested prestige in being older and many well-meaning parents will be down-right coercive in their conversations and political discussions with their offspring, and that the whole will have a rebound effect."

"I think I can speak for my age," he said. "If someone told me to do one thing to the point of being obnoxious, and I saw no great harm in doing the opposite, I would tend to do the opposite."

He hopes adults won't "tend to be overly zealous of their own prestige in matters of decision and fail to recognize legitimate points of someone younger than they, because of some sort of tribal pecking order, shall we say."

The California legislature is reviewing the state vote for 18-year-olds, and if there isn't some clarification and/or state constitutional amendment, it may be necessary to have separate ballots for 18–19–20-year-olds.

Los Angeles Councilman Thomas Bradley, the day following the Supreme Court action, called upon the California legislature to give all 18-year-olds the right to vote in all state and local elections, beginning with the general election in 1972.

Three of the 50 states have a minimum voting age of 18— Alaska, Georgia and Kentucky, Montana and Massachusetts have a 19-year-old vote, and Maine, Nebraska and Hawaii, 20-year-old.

The Supreme Court's 5-4 decision in December [1970] upholding the 18-year-old vote for presidential and congressional elections will open the door to voting to more than 10 million young persons.

The States Are Being Extorted into Ratifying the Twenty-sixth Amendment

James J. Kilpatrick

James J. Kilpatrick is a well-known political columnist and has been a debater on the television programs 60 Minutes *and* Meet the Press. *He is the author of several books. In the following viewpoint he argues that the Supreme Court's ruling that congressional lowering of the voting age is valid for federal, but not state, elections was a violation of the Constitution. Furthermore, he says, it amounts to extortion, because the states are being forced to ratify a constitutional amendment to lower the voting age or else keep two sets of registration books. It is wrong, in his opinion, to put the states in this impossible position, which in some cases will mean they must approve a proposition that their own people have previously rejected.*

The House of Representatives [in late March 1971] completed congressional action on a constitutional amendment extending the vote to young men and women at age 18. Within hours, Minnesota, Delaware, Tennessee, Connecticut and Washington had ratified. The rush is on.

It is an exercise in futility to voice dissent in the midst of a bandwagon's brassy roar; but such an exercise may be useful all the same. To extort, by definition, is to obtain some object "by force or undue or illegal power or ingenuity." What we are engaged in here, by the grace of Congress and the whim of Supreme Court Justice Hugo Black, precisely fits that definition. What it is, is extortion.

This crime against the Constitution began [in 1970], when Congress undertook by simple statute to extend the vote to

Ratification of the 26th Amendment and Earlier State Action on Lowering the Voting Age

The 26th Amendment was proposed three months after the Supreme Court ruled that Congress could not set the voting age for state or local elections, and was ratified in only 100 days—faster than any other amendment to the Constitution. Some states had already considered measures to lower the voting age. This table shows whether or not those earlier measures passed.

State	Date Ratified	Earlier
Alabama	June 30, 1971	NA
Alaska	April 8, 1971	Yes (1959)
Arizona	May 14, 1971	NA
Arkansas	March 30, 1971	NA
California	April 19, 1971	NA
Colorado	April 27, 1971	No (1970)
Connecticut	March 23, 1971	No (1970)
Delaware	March 23, 1971	NA
Florida	NA	No (1970)
Georgia	October 4, 1971	Yes (1943)
Hawaii	March 24, 1971	Yes (1959)
Idaho	March 30, 1971	No (1960)
Illinois	June 29, 1971	No (1970)
Indiana	April 8, 1971	NA
Iowa	March 30, 1971	NA
Kansas	April 7, 1971	Yes (1971)
Kentucky	NA	Yes (1955)
Louisiana	April 17, 1971	NA
Maine	April 9, 1971	Yes (1970)
Maryland	April 8, 1971	No (1968)
Massachusetts	March 24, 1971	Yes (1970)
Michigan	April 7, 1971	No (1966)
Minnesota	March 23, 1971	Yes (1970)
Mississippi	NA	NA
Missouri	June 14, 1971	NA
Montana	March 29, 1971	Yes (1970)
Nebraska	April 2, 1971	Yes (1970)

[CONTINUED]

[CONTINUED]

Ratification of the 26th Amendment and Earlier State Action on Lowering the Voting Age

The 26th Amendment was proposed three months after the Supreme Court ruled that Congress could not set the voting age for state or local elections, and was ratified in only 100 days—faster than any other amendment to the Constitution. Some states had already considered measures to lower the voting age. This table shows whether or not those earlier measures passed.

State	Date Ratified	Earlier
Nevada	NA	Yes (1971)
New Hampshire	May 13, 1971	NA
New Jersey	April 3, 1971	No (1969)
New Mexico	NA	NA
New York	June 2, 1971	No (1970)
North Carolina	July 1, 1971	NA
North Dakota	NA	No (1968)
Ohio	June 30, 1971	No (1969)
Oklahoma	July 1, 1971	No (1952)
Oregon	June 4, 1971	No (1970)
Pennsylvania	April 27, 1971	NA
Rhode Island	May 27, 1971	NA
South Carolina	April 28, 1971	NA
South Dakota	NA	No (1970)
Tennessee	March 23, 1971	No (1968)
Texas	April 27, 1971	NA
Utah	NA	NA
Vermont	April 16, 1971	NA
Virginia	July 8, 1971	NA
Washington	March 23, 1971	No (1970)
West Virginia	April 28, 1971	NA
Wisconsin	June 22, 1971	NA
Wyoming	July 8, 1971	No (1970)

TAKEN FROM: Compiled by editor.

18-year-olds in all elections. [President Richard] Nixon, against his better judgment, signed the bill. A test case, challenging the act, went to the Supreme Court in October. In December, the Court split 5-4, in one of the most bizarre decisions in its history, holding the law valid in part and void in part.

Mr. Justice Black was the swing man. The aging Alabaman agreed with the Court's conservatives that Congress had no power to fix a minimum age for voting in elections to state offices; but he flopped to the liberals in ruling that Congress may exert its will as to national offices. His reasoning, if so it may be termed, went along these lines: Congress has power, under the Constitution, to make its own regulations or to alter state regulations prescribing "the manner of holding elections for senators and representatives." The word "manner," Black decided, embraces the minimum age of voters. And though the provision is limited explicitly to senators and representatives, Black ruled that the provision is just bound to apply to the election of Presidents also. The deed was done.

Chaos for the States

The result was not only to rape the Constitution but also to create chaos for the states. Election officials in 47 states—all but Alaska, Georgia and Kentucky, which already have fixed a minimum age of 18 by their own action—face the expense of maintaining two sets of registration books, one for state elections, the other for national elections.

To eliminate this costly and confusing prospect, the Congress now has approved a proposed 26th Amendment to the Constitution. The resolution is clumsily worded, but the intent is plain:

"The right of citizens of the United States who are 18 years of age or older, to vote shall not be denied or abridged by the United States or by any state on account of age. The Congress shall have power to enforce this article by appropriate legislation."

That is the proposition sent forth [in March] for ratification. If 38 states agree within a seven-year period, the amendment will become part of the Constitution.

Whatever the law may be, it is wrong—simply wrong—for the states to be put in this impossible position. The legislatures are not free to consider the proposal on its merits. They are being told to ratify or else—or else face the chaos and expense of two sets of books. Probably the states will cave in; but many of them, in doing so, will act against the expressed will of their own voters. The people of Connecticut, for one example, rejected a state proposal to lower the age to 18; but now Connecticut's General Assembly has ratified the amendment.

Connecticut's voters are not alone. The people of nine other states rejected lower-than-21 proposals. In all of them, the state legislatures face the uncomfortable prospect of approving a proposition their own people have specifically disapproved.

It has to be acknowledged, again, that doubtless it is futile to protest at this point, but the states, if they value the integrity of the amendatory process, should refuse even to consider ratification until Congress has first repealed its own 18-year-old statute. This would free the states from extortion. In the blessed name of federalism, it seems little enough to ask.

The Majority of Americans Favor the Twenty-sixth Amendment

George Gallup

George Gallup was the founder of the Gallup Organization, which regularly conducts polls on different topics and reports the results. The poll discussed in the following viewpoint was conducted in April 1971, when nearly half the states had already ratified the Twenty-sixth Amendment. It showed that six in ten Americans favored lowering the voting age to eighteen for state and local elections. More than eight in ten eighteen- to twenty-year olds favored it. However, among people over fifty, approval outweighed disapproval by only a narrow margin. Most people interviewed for the poll who favored letting young people vote said that if they were old enough to fight they should be allowed to vote and that they were well informed and qualified to do so. Those opposed argued that people between eighteen and twenty were not mature enough or well enough informed. The Supreme Court ruling allowing them to vote in federal elections created potential problems for the Republican Party because surveys had shown that the Democratic Party's views were favored by young people.

Six in 10 Americans favor lowering the voting age to 18 for local and state elections, with a majority in each of the four major regions of the nation expressing approval.

As might be expected, a high proportion (more than eight in 10) of 18-to-20-year olds favor lowering the voting age to 18 for local and state elections.

However, considerable opposition to such a change is found among Republicans and older persons (50 and over), with approval outweighing disapproval by a relatively narrow margin.

Only 17% of all persons interviewed favored lowering the voting age to 18 when the Gallup Poll first sought the public's views on this subject, in 1939.

Separate Registrations Would Be Costly

The U.S. Supreme Court ruled in December [1970] that the voting age be lowered to 18 for federal or national elections. However, since the ruling applies only to federal elections, a constitutional amendment is now being presented to the 50 states which would extend the 18-year-old vote to local and state elections, as well.

One of the chief arguments for lowering the voting age in local and state elections is an economic one. If the 1970 law applied only to national elections, most states would have to maintain separate registration and voting procedures for the different types of elections, at an estimated cost of $20 million.

To go into effect, the proposed constitutional amendment must be ratified by three-fourths of the states.

As of this writing, the measure has been approved by 20 states.

Should the states fail to ratify the federal amendment, individual states could still lower the voting age by referendum or legislative action.

Poll Results

For the survey reported today, a total of 1,550 adults, 18 and older, were interviewed in person in more than 300 scientifically selected localities across the nation. Interviewing was conducted April 3, 4 and 5 [1971]. This question was asked.

Gallup Poll Results			
	Favor	Oppose	No opinion
National	60%	33%	5%
East	62	31	7
Midwest	54	41	5
South	65	31	4
Far West	57	38	5
Republicans	50	44	6
Democrats	63	32	5
Independents	64	32	4
18–20 years	84	14	2
21–29 years	73	21	6
30–49 years	57	38	3
50 & over	52	41	7

TAKEN FROM: George Gallup, "60% Back Full Vote for Youths," April 25, 1971.

The Supreme Court has ruled that the voting age be lowered to 18 for federal or national elections. Do you favor or oppose lowering the voting age to 18 for local and state elections?

[The table includes] the national results, and those by region, party affiliation and age.

Persons interviewed who favor lowering the voting age most frequently give these reasons: (1) If young people are old enough to fight, they are old enough to vote; (2) people in the 18 to 20 age group are well informed, qualified to vote; and, (3) they should have a say in how the country is run.

Those who oppose lowering the voting age argue that young people are: (1) Not mature enough to cast a responsible vote; and, (2) are not well enough informed about the issues.

As reported earlier, the U.S. Supreme Court ruling, which gives the vote to 11 million Americans in federal elections, could cause serious problems for the Republican Party. Recent surveys show the Democratic Party holding marked advantages among this age group in terms of political party allegiance, attitudes toward the war and the [Richard M.] Nixon Administration, and support for Democrats in trial heats against President Nixon.

The Effect of Young Voters on Politics Is Unpredictable

David S. Broder

David S. Broder was a staff writer for the Washington Post *when he wrote the following article and is now a* Post *political columnist. The article was written a few days after the ratification of the Twenty-sixth Amendment. Broder points out that when women won the right to vote there was no impact on American politics and considers the question of whether the impact of young voters will be greater. Political analysts disagree about this, he says, but opinion is swinging toward the view that eighteen- to twenty-year-olds may constitute an important electoral force. The number of potential new voters is very large, but past history shows that the proportion of people who vote increases with age. Registration drives have so far reached a low proportion of under-21s, except in high schools that have held assemblies with registrars present. As to how young people will vote, many analysts believe they will follow family traditions, but on the other hand, polls show that there are significant differences between generations. More young people consider themselves independents, and of those who choose a party, more are registering as Democrats. The majority of young people do not want President Richard Nixon to be reelected, largely because of their opposition to the Vietnam War. Nevertheless, it is uncertain how much actual effect new voters will have on the outcome of the 1972 election.*

In 1920, after a half-century of struggle, the women of America won the right to vote—through the ratification of the 19th Amendment to the Constitution. Overnight, the number of potential voters doubled. And nothing happened in American politics.

The long era of Republican dominance—broken only by Woodrow Wilson's two narrow victories—continued until the Depression came along to alter the political orientation of men and women alike.

Last week [in June 1971] Ohio's legislature completed the process of ratifying the 26th Amendment—granting the franchise in all elections to 18-, 19- and 20-year-olds.

Will this addition to the electorate—the biggest potential increase since women won the franchise half a century ago—make any more difference than the women's vote?

There are as many guesses as there are self-styled political experts. Former Democratic Rep. Allard K. Lowenstein of New York, who is running one of the many efforts to enroll young people as voters, tells his registration rallies that they have the power to end the war, defeat Richard M. Nixon and replace him in the White House with a more palatable President from either party.

On the other hand, Attorney General John N. Mitchell, who is likely to direct Mr. Nixon's reelection bid, says he sees no reason to make the new voters a special political objective. Expressing his skepticism that the well-publicized campus activists speak for their contemporaries, Mitchell says Republicans can do as well with young voters as with any segment of the population.

Among more detached observers, the consensus has begun to swing from the view that the young voters will likely echo their parents' political opinions—but turn out in lesser numbers—to the view that they may constitute an important and independent electoral force.

Registration efforts—which so far have reached but a small fraction of the potential new vote—turn up disproportionately large Democratic margins. Polls have shown the young people more antiwar, anti-Nixon and liberal on social and racial issues than older voters.

LuAnne Simpson, seventeen, of Dover, N.H., meets with Rep. Paul N. McCloskey of California (center) and actor Paul Newman as they campaign in Dover, March 6, 1972, a few days before Simpson's eighteenth birthday. AP Images.

Analysts' Views

Political analyst Richard M. Scammon argued in a 1970 book that if the 18- through 20-year-olds had been able to vote in 1968, and had voted in the same percentages as those just a little older did, the outcome of the presidential election would have been unchanged in all 50 states.

Now, however, Scammon is beginning to hedge his bets. He conceded in a recent discussion that the young people may be "moderately more Democratic" than their parents, and said that if the election is as close as the one in 1968, "even a small difference could change the outcome." Samuel Lubell, another respected political analyst, is bolder, predicting in *Look* magazine that "the 18-year-old vote could beat Nixon in 1972."

On the other hand, there are counter-currents, including the fact that polls show the new voters far more favorable to George Wallace than their elders and the fact that many of the youths say they are "independents," up for grabs depending on what the final choice of candidates is.

The uncertainty about the final impact of this potential new vote is heightened by the fact that at least three separate questions must be answered to make a prediction of any validity: How many will vote? Where will they vote? And how will they vote?

As to the first question, the raw numbers are very impressive. The Census Bureau says there are 11.2 million 18-through 20-year olds in the country. The group includes about 4 million college students, 4.1 million full-time workers, 1 million housewives, 900,000 high school students and about 800,000 members of the armed forces.

When they are added to the almost 14 million young people who have turned 21 since the last election, the total number of newly eligible voters for 1972 climbs to 25.1 million—more than one-sixth of the total potential electorate.

The number of potential first-time presidential voters is almost 50 times as great as Mr. Nixon's half million popular-vote margin over Hubert H. Humphrey in 1968. The number of potential new voters dwarfs the winning candidate's margin in all 50 states and the District of Columbia.

The process of enfranchising the 18-year-olds began with passage of the Voting Rights Act of 1970. The Supreme Court upheld the constitutionality of the statute but limited its application to elections for federal office—president, vice president, senator and representative. Thereafter, Congress approved a constitutional amendment extending the 18-year-old franchise to all elections, and the legislatures completed ratification in record time.

The first widespread test of the new vote will come this autumn [1971], with municipal elections in Philadelphia, Boston and other major cities, election of a lieutenant governor in Virginia, of governors in Kentucky, Louisiana, and Mississippi and a legislature in New Jersey.

1972 Conventions

Next year, the test will reach into every state, not just in the general election but in the primaries and in local and state conventions—all of which are now open to teenagers. Indeed, Democratic Party rules reforms require that young people—defined as 18- to 30-year olds—be represented in reasonable proportion in the national convention itself. Massachusetts Attorney General Robert H. Quinn has ruled that the new amendment makes any 18-year-old resident of the commonwealth eligible to be governor, since the state constitution specifies no special age for the office.

If the door is wide open for youths' participation, there is as yet no real evidence how many of them will choose to avail themselves of the opportunity.

Past history indicates that a significantly smaller proportion of young people take part in elections than older voters. Only 41 percent of persons 21 to 29 years old reported to the Census Bureau that they voted in 1970. This is in contrast to the report of those in the 55-and-up age bracket, of whom 65 percent say they voted. Fifty-one percent of the 30-to-34 year olds say they voted in 1970, while an average of 61 percent of the people in the 25-to-54 age bracket report that they cast their ballots.

In the four states that allowed 18-year-olds to vote in 1970—Georgia, Kentucky, Alaska and Hawaii—only 25 percent of under 21-year-olds voted, while 55 percent of the over-21s turned out at the polls.

Greater transiency among the young people and the lesser stake in community affairs are the reasons usually cited for that low turnout. Some observers believe that the lure of a presidential contest—particularly their first presidential contest—will bring many more of them to the polls.

Registration Drives

The evidence of the registration drives so far undertaken is contradictory—but inconclusive—on this point. Dozens of different groups are working in the field, including both parties, a variety of union-sponsored organizations, and many citizens groups, including John Gardner's Common Cause.

In some instances, where high schools have held special assemblies for 18-year-old students with deputy registrars present, two-thirds or more of the potential voters have been registered on the spot. But as an official of the Youth Citizenship Fund, Inc., one of the groups involved in these projects, has commented, "High school students are the most eager and the easiest to register." Community-wide and statewide registration drives have netted much lower percentages—about 18 percent in New York City and about 16 percent in Massachusetts.

Sponsors point out that these drives were undertaken at a low point of interest in the elections, and they expect much better results when they resume their work in the fall. Many of the planned campaigns focus on the college and high school students—who comprise less than half of the potential new under-21 voters.

"Invisible Youth"

A major worry for all these groups is locating and enrolled what Charlotte Kemble of Frontlash, a union-backed registration group, calls "the invisible youth," the workers, the housewives, the unemployed. "Mainly the activist youths are registering now," she said, "and no one's getting at the hard-core, less-motivated and less educated youths."

One simple device for reaching the male half of the youth voters was put forward by Sen. Thomas F. Eagleton (D-Mo.). Eagleton managed to add an amendment to the draft bill extension in the Senate, providing that as each 18-year-old registered with his local Selective Service board, he would automatically be registered at the same time as a voter. However, the Eagleton amendment has been knocked out of the measure by House-Senate conferees, and the problem of getting young people to register remains unsolved.

Residency Rules

Closely related to the question of who will vote is the matter of where they will vote.

The Common Cause voting rights project is coordinating a number of legal challenges to state laws restricting voting by students and other minors at their place of residence—whether it be a college dormitory or boarding house—and requiring instead that they vote in their parents' home precinct. Lawsuits challenging such restrictions have been filed or are planned in Alabama, California, Connecticut, Kentucky, Massachusetts, Michigan, Minnesota, New Jersey, New York, North Carolina, Ohio, Tennessee, and Wisconsin.

Those challenging the statutes and rulings claim it is discriminatory and unfair to a require a 20-year-old unmarried steelworker in Oakland, for example, to return to his parents' home in San Diego or to cast an absentee ballot in order to vote. Equally unjust, they say, is the Massachusetts law which requires a 19-year-old Harvard student whose parents live in Tennessee to register and vote in their home precinct. Cumbersome procedures for absentee registration and voting, they assert, will substantially reduce the number of young people who take part in the elections.

On the other hand, many local politicians are vehemently opposed to the enfranchisement of the massive student populations in small college towns. They assert that the Michigan State University student body could well take control of East Lansing, even though most of them have only a transient interest in the city's affairs and few of them pay any local taxes.

Their argument highlights one often-neglected aspect of the youth vote. Whatever the impact on the presidential contest, it could well be decisive in local races—particularly if the pending court tests open the way for the 4 million college students to vote from their campus residences.

Unknown Factors

The question of how the young voters will vote next year obviously depends on several unknown factors—including the identity of the candidates and the number of the potential new voters who actually get to the polls. The available data about their political dispositions offers contradictory clues—but points to the likelihood of some net benefit to the Democrats.

Most political science texts stress the continuity of voting traditions within a family. University of Michigan Survey Research Center scholars, in their classic study, *The American Voter*, show that generational differences are much less important determinants of voting behavior than family background and socio-economic status.

Scammon, in a recent talk on a conference on youth registration, emphasized that "young people are not at all monolithic in their political views."

"The fact of the matter is," he said, "there is less of a generation gap in America than there is a class gap. The working-class kid from the Italian-American half of Cambridge, [Massachusetts,] the kid whose father is working as a fry cook in a White Tower [fast-food restaurant], has more in common with his father than he does with the undergraduate at Harvard University from a psychiatrist's family in Scarsdale."

What Polls Show

All this sounds plausible enough, and it has the backing of precedent. But there are also reputable public opinion studies which show significant differences between the under-21 voters and their elders.

The Gallup Poll in April [1971] gave Democrats a 42 per cent to 18 per cent lead over the Republicans among the under-21 voters; the Harris Survey in January [1971] put the Democrats' lead at 38 per cent to 14 per cent. The Democrats' margin among the young people was only a third to one-half greater than among the older voters. Both polls showed the proportion calling themselves independents or undecided was significantly higher among the young people—about two of every five under-21s fitting that category, while only one-quarter of the older voters so classified themselves.

Those findings are confirmed by the scattered registration figures so far available. Preliminary returns from California show a 3-to-1 Democratic-over-Republican advantage, while registration of adults leans only 5-to-4 Democratic. Pennsylvania reported a 2-to-1 Democratic margin and in some high schools and colleges the ratio has been as high as 5-to-1.

Even persons working for liberal organizations are skeptical that these registration figures guarantee such an advantage to Democrats at election time. Most are inclined to believe that high proportions of young people are genuinely independent or undecided, and are registering Democratic largely because they believe "that's where the action will be" in next year's presidential primaries.

However, there is little comfort for Mr. Nixon in any of the available studies. Gallup and Harris show 7 percent and 12 percent fewer young people, respectively, approve of Mr. Nixon's handling of his job than do the older voters—and both polls put his popularity figure well below the 50 percent mark.

Trial Heats

Lubell, in his magazine article, said that "of the sons and daughters of Republican parents interviewed in colleges, high schools and youth organizations across the country, more than a third do not want Nixon reelected. Less than a tenth of their classmates from Democratic families are swinging to Nixon."

Their dissatisfaction with the President appears closely linked to their vehement opposition to the Vietnam war. Every survey has shown young people more anxious than their elders to withdraw all U.S. troops from Vietnam this year, and less tolerant of Mr. Nixon's slower-paced withdrawal.

How much of their opposition he can overcome if he manages to end the war before election day is uncertain. Similarly uncertain—and important—is how far Mr. Nixon can cut into the sizeable youth vote for third-party candidate George Wallace. The Gallup Poll shows the Alabama governor with 20 percent of the under-21 vote in some trial heats—a testament, perhaps, to the genuineness of the young people's independent streak.

When the Youth Vote Was Young: Student Voters Had More Impact on Local Elections than on National Elections

Clyde Brown and Gayle K. Pluta Brown

Clyde Brown is a professor of political science at Miami University in Ohio, and Gayle K. Pluta Brown has a Ph.D. in history from the University of Iowa. In the following article they discuss the first test of the impact of the youth vote in Iowa following adoption of the Twenty-sixth Amendment. Students at Iowa's three public universities were active in the 1971 local elections, and one of them was elected mayor of Cedar Falls. In Ames, Iowa, the student vote was the deciding factor in the election of two city council members, and in Iowa City students' votes contributed to the success of one candidate and came close to achieving the election of two others. In contrast, the youth vote did not have much effect on the 1972 national election or in subsequent ones. The Browns conclude that national elections are not where student voters have an impact; it is in local elections where their concentrated numbers give them an advantage, provided that they are politically mobilized.

At the end of June 1971 the 26th Amendment became part of the United States Constitution. It gave 18-to-20-year-olds, including 160,000 Iowans, the right to vote in federal, state, and local elections. The Amendment came at the end of a controversial decade of student activism and put to rest an issue that had been around since the nation's founding. . . .

Clyde Brown and Gayle K. Pluta Brown, "Iowa University Towns and the 26th Amendment: The First Test of the Newly Enfranchised Student Vote in 1971," April 15, 2004, pp. 1–6, 19–20. Reproduced by permission of the authors and the State Historical Society of Iowa, publisher of The Annals of Iowa. www.allacademic.com/meta/p83586_index.html.

The first real opportunity for young Iowans to exercise their new right came in the November 1971 local elections. In Iowa City, where anti-Vietnam War protests had started earliest, been the most confrontational, and engaged the largest number of students, none of the five student candidates survived the primary, but one student-endorsed candidate won in the General Election. In Ames, [Iowa,] anger over treatment of student protesters during May 1970 antiwar demonstrations fueled activists' efforts to register their fellow students and get them to the polls to ensure victory for the students' chosen candidates. And in Cedar Falls, [Iowa,] UNI [University of Northern Iowa] graduate student Jon Crews was elected mayor. He went on to win nine more terms and remains mayor today [in 2004].

Student Activism

Colleges and universities throughout the United States coped with increasing enrollments and an increasingly restive student body during the 1960s. Students called for changes in campus rules governing student behavior such as dormitory curfews. They demanded a more relevant curriculum and pressed for the right to evaluate instructors. The civil rights movement came to campus as African-Americans called for increases in the number of minority students and faculty and lobbied for the establishment of African-American Studies programs and student centers. Feminists did the same, asking for more women faculty to be hired and for Women's Studies programs and women's centers on campus. By the end of the decade homosexuals were coming together in their own Gay Rights movement and widespread concern over air and water pollution and wildlife extinction led to the establishment of an environmental movement. But it was opposition to the Vietnam War that engaged the largest number of students and the antiwar protester who became the symbol of 1960s student activism in the popular mind.

Iowa's three public universities were not exempt from the upheaval that hit campuses in the 1960s. Violent antiwar protests at the University of Iowa led to arson, vandalism on and off campus, attempts to block traffic on city streets and highways, and battles with counter-demonstrators. Because of the student outbursts city and university officials brought outside law enforcement officers to Iowa City to supplement local and university police in November 1967, May 1970, and May 1971. Nonviolence prevailed at Iowa State's antiwar rallies and marches with none of the destructive behavior seen at UI [University of Iowa]. Where hundreds of University of Iowa students were arrested at protests over the years at ISU [Iowa State University] less than fifty went to jail, all in connection with two sit-ins in May 1970 protesting the Cambodian invasion. . . . At all three schools, the Vietnam Moratorium in fall 1969 and demonstrations following the Cambodian invasion and the student killings at Kent State University and Jackson State College in May 1970 brought out the largest number of student protesters.

In addition to protest, young people in the 1960s, many energized by the election and inaugural address of President John F. Kennedy, became active in electoral politics. Not surprisingly, as student opposition to the Vietnam War increased, they gave their allegiance to candidates pledged to ending the war, most notably the presidential campaigns of Senators Eugene McCarthy (D-Minnesota) and Robert Kennedy (D-New York) in 1968. McCarthy's campaign, dubbed the "children's crusade," attracted legions of young people even though many volunteers and staffers were not old enough to vote.

The political upheaval of the 1960s, including the bitter controversy over U.S. involvement in Vietnam, led to the revival of efforts to lower the voting age to eighteen. Proposals to lower the voting age were put forward "during or after every major war" as far back as the American Revolution by proponents who argued that if young soldiers were old enough to fight they were old enough to vote. The Vietnam War provided a new twist on that argument. Far from simply rewarding the sacrifices of military men between the ages of eighteen and twenty, the franchise would give youthful opponents of the war the opportunity to vote for politicians who wanted to end the fighting. . . .

The 26th Amendment officially became part of the Constitution July 5, 1971. Over eleven million 18-to-20-year-olds now had the right to vote in federal, state and local elections.

After passage of the 26th Amendment, state and local officials had to decide whether to allow college students to register and vote in the community where they attended school. This was a controversial issue because student voters outnumbered permanent residents in some college towns. Incumbents worried that the youngsters would vote them out of office. Residents feared higher taxes if student voters passed expensive bond issues or elected free-spending city councils and school boards, and Republicans worried that Democratically-inclined young people would end their party's political dominance in certain communities. . . .

Voting in Local Elections

The decisions to participate in an election and whom to cast one's ballot(s) for are well-studied, but complex phenomena. Both acts involve interplay between electoral rules, the individual voter, the candidates, and other political actors. . . .

Citizens have to register before they can vote in an election. In the United States, unlike most other western-style democracies, the onus [responsibility] is on the individual to take the bureaucratic step to become registered. The argument in favor of registering voters is that it prevents voter fraud. While it accomplishes that purpose, it also undeniably reduces voter participation by creating a prerequisite for voting. At the time of the events described in this [article], long before postcard and email voter registration, and before the Motor Voter

Voting-Age Population, Percent Reporting Registered and Voted: 1972 to 2006

	Age 18 to 24		Age 25 to 44		Age 45 to 64		Age 65 and up	
	Registered	Voted	Registered	Voted	Registered	Voted	Registered	Voted
1972	58.9	49.6	71.3	62.7	79.7	70.8	75.6	63.5
1974	41.3	23.8	59.9	42.2	73.6	56.9	70.2	51.4
1976	51.3	42.2	65.5	58.7	75.5	68.7	71.4	62.2
1978	40.5	23.5	60.2	43.1	74.3	58.5	72.8	55.9
1980	49.2	39.9	65.6	58.7	75.8	69.3	74.6	65.1
1982	42.4	24.8	61.5	45.4	75.6	62.2	75.2	59.9
1984	51.3	40.8	66.6	58.4	76.6	69.8	76.9	67.7
1986	42.0	21.9	61.1	41.4	74.8	58.7	76.9	60.9
1988	48.2	36.2	63.0	54.0	75.5	67.9	78.4	68.8

[CONTINUED]

[CONTINUED]

Voting-Age Population, Percent Reporting Registered and Voted: 1972 to 2006

	Age 18 to 24		Age 25 to 44		Age 45 to 64		Age 65 and up	
	Registered	Voted	Registered	Voted	Registered	Voted	Registered	Voted
1990	39.9	20.4	58.4	40.7	71.4	55.8	76.5	60.3
1992	52.5	42.8	64.8	58.3	75.3	70.0	78.0	70.1
1994	42.3	20.1	57.9	39.4	71.7	56.7	76.3	61.3
1996	48.8	32.4	61.9	49.2	73.5	64.4	77.0	67.0
1998	39.2	16.6	57.7	34.8	71.1	53.6	75.4	59.5
2000	45.4	32.3	59.6	49.8	71.2	64.1	76.1	67.6
2002	38.2	17.2	55.4	34.1	69.4	53.1	75.8	61.0
2004	51.5	41.9	60.1	52.2	72.7	66.6	76.9	68.9
2006	41.6	19.9	55.0	34.4	69.6	54.3	75.4	60.5

TAKEN FROM: U.S. Census Bureau.

Act of 1993 [the National Voter Registration Act, which made the registration process easier], voter registration requirements were a significant institutional barrier to voter participation.

Some individuals are sufficiently self-motivated to register and vote; others are not. It is known that high socio-economic (SES) individuals are more likely to take these steps than low SES individuals. One component of SES is an individual's level of education, a characteristic that college students rate high on in comparison to others in society. But college students are younger than other voters and usually have fewer ties to the community where they are residing, both factors that make it less likely that an individual will participate in local elections. Also, by definition, 18-to-20-year-olds have not developed the "habit" of voting which recent studies of American elections have shown to be important. Furthermore, voter registration deadlines several weeks before Election Day make it likely that many citizens will not be foresighted enough to register on time. Because of these impediments to registering and voting, election organizations and activists, if they have the capacity, engage in mobilization efforts to encourage and facilitate the participation of voters who would not participate on their own. Political mobilization of all kinds—registering citizens to vote, providing voters with information, and contacting voters by various means to encourage voting—has been shown to increase political participation.

Political Mobilization

Political mobilization can also influence how a voter votes. It is not the only consideration, but it can be a very important one under certain conditions. Other factors can be important, such as an individual's political party affiliation if it is a partisan election (President of the United States), candidate characteristics (photogenic or not, likeability factor, celebrity status, gender, ethnicity, etc.), and salient issues (war and peace, the economy, crime, NIMBY-issues ["Not In My Back Yard"—

opposition to local development viewed as undesirable], etc.). Nonpartisan elections lack the voting cue, i.e., party label, that political scientists have identified as being the most important vote determinant and, as a consequence, increase the possibility that other "cues" will become important. Candidates and issues are short-term factors that vary by election and office. Political mobilization is not a purely mechanical task; all political mobilization is not equal. To be effective political activists must have credibility in the eyes of those they hope to influence and research has shown that messages from political elites to voters for support will be more effective if they don't have to compete with conflicting messages from other elites.

Political mobilization does not occur out of the goodness of anyone's heart; rather it takes place for purposes of political advantage. Activists make the effort because they believe it will gain them votes on Election Day. It is relatively rare to blindly mobilize demographic groups of people because individuals in a complex society such as the United States usually do not vote in lock-step fashion; voters are not as uniform in their interests and experiences as a first glance often makes it appear. Block voting by socio-demographic groups, referred to as reference group effects, is not usually much of a factor in American elections. Yet that is what activists in the wake of ratification of the 26th Amendment attempted to do. They were trying to get out the "student vote" in the expectation that students would vote en masse for an antiwar candidate. [Democratic politician] Allard Lowenstein and others sought to mobilize young voters, especially college students, nationwide to defeat President Nixon. In 1971 university students were an ideal cohort for political mobilization. They were relatively homogenous in their socio-demographic characteristics, they shared common life experiences (including traumatic events like the protests that followed the U.S. invasion of Cambodia in 1970) and a similar youth culture, many of them felt threatened by and therefore opposed to the Vietnam

War and favored the nascent environmental and women's movement developing at the time, they lived in close geographical proximity to each other, some, especially antiwar leaders had unsatisfactory experiences with social control agents, and they had established channels of communication within their student communities. The student activists involved in the elections in Ames, Cedar Falls, and Iowa City sought to involve their fellow students across the board in winning local political power to further their interests. . . .

Several factors came together in 1971 to allow ISU students to have a decisive impact on the November election. First, a small group of antiwar activists, nursing a grievance against the city attorney for his treatment of demonstrators in May 1970, were ready to work to elect members of the city council pledged to remove him from office. Second, a larger group of activists, energized by Lowenstein's Register for Peace Conference, were motivated to add their fellow students to the voter rolls to increase student voting power in the fall election. And finally, older activists were on hand to give the students advice on choosing viable candidates and running a labor-intensive door-to-door local election campaign. . . .

Electoral Power

Students at ISU, UNI, and UI all took advantage of the opportunity provided by the 26th Amendment's dramatic expansion of the electorate to effect local politics. The November 1971 municipal elections were in essence the first test of the newly enfranchised cohort's electoral power in Iowa. The extent of those efforts and the results achieved varied across the three towns, with some degree of success achieved in all three locations. . . .

The candidacy of students for city council played out differently in the three cities. Students were most active in this regard in Iowa City where five candidates were forthcoming. It is probable that the large number of candidates divided the student vote preventing any of the five from surviving the primary. In Cedar Falls, a graduate student who had worked actively in the past to register college students to impact local elections ran for city office without calling much attention to his status as a college student. Undoubtedly, he felt emphasizing this characteristic would harm his chances with other constituencies in Cedar Falls. At ISU a conscious choice was made by student organizers not to run student candidates, but instead to recruit a like-minded older member of the Ames community to run for each local office deemed winnable on Election Day. The strategy of endorsing a slate of non-student candidates was only done in Ames and it proved very successful.

The difference between winning and losing an election often hinges of the strength of political mobilization organizations working at the grassroots level. Besides registering voters before an election, such organizations contact prospective voters to provide information (voting cues) and urge support for endorsed candidates, identify the vote intention of prospective voters, and remind prospective voters leaning towards their favored candidates to vote on Election Day. Candidate organizations and political parties often perform these functions. Here the focus is on non-candidate and non-party organizations and whether they played a significant role in the three city elections.

All three campuses and communities had organizations, such as the three university student governments and the League of Women Voters, which made efforts to register students. However, only one campus had an organization that completed the other tasks involved in a full political mobilization effort. That organization was the Coalition for Responsive City Government (CRCG) in Ames. The CRCG endorsed a slate of candidates, contacted registered student voters to provide them with information about CRCG and its endorsed candidates, delivered reminders to potential voters the day before the election, monitored voter participation by means of poll watchers on Election Day, and conducted a voter contact effort on Election Day to urge students who had not yet voted to do so before the polls closed. It is clear from the record that the CRCG's efforts were a major reason why the student-endorsed slate of candidates won election to the Ames City Council. This was not the case in Iowa City or Cedar Falls where comparable organizations did not exist. . . .

Political mobilizing is hard work. Political science does not know exactly why some people chose to be political activists. It is reasonable to conclude that there was a generalized belief across the board in the minds of political mobilizers that university students were more progressive and liberal in their political views than the adult voting population of the three towns. ISU, UNI, and UI student activists all complained about the operation of city hall and called for more responsive and representative governments. In addition in Ames and Iowa City (at least during the primary contest) there were specific complaints related to the steps local officials took to control student protests against the Vietnam War. Objections to the behavior of law enforcement officials became the central focus of the coalition of students who organized and supported the CRCG in Ames. In Iowa City, during the primary, most of the student candidates and some other candidates voiced concern about the police response to the May 1971 protests, but that issue seemed to disappear by the time of the general election.

Impact of the Youth Vote

The youth vote in the three college towns had a significant impact on the city elections in 1971. It was the deciding factor in the election of two city councilors and boosted the political prestige of a third in Ames. In Iowa City, it contributed to the victory of one city council member while coming close, but failing, to get two others over the top. And in Cedar Falls, a fellow student was elected convincingly to the highest city office. In politics, where "you win some, you lose some," the student vote passed its first test in a fairly impressive fashion.

Despite some initial indications of student power at the ballot box in 1971 such as those documented in this manuscript, Lowenstein's ambitious goal of a bipartisan youth movement capable of impacting the 1972 presidential elections was not achieved. Beginning with George McGovern's loss to Richard Nixon, the youth vote has not had a significant impact on national elections. Students of political behavior have noted the failure of 18-to-20-year-olds as a group to utilize the franchise fully. Young voters vote less often than any other age cohort in America. (The situation is not as bad for college students who vote twice as often as 18-to-20-year-olds as a group.) For national elections, the downward slide began with the 1974 congressional elections and shows no sign of letting up.

But national politics is not where student voters can have a substantial impact; local politics is where their concentrated numbers give them an advantage. Reliable figures by demographic characteristics, such as age cohort, for local elections in the United States do not exist. However, it is a sure bet given the low levels of participation by all age groups in such elections that young people vote even less in city elections than they do in national elections. But student voters in Ames, as well as Cedar Falls and Iowa City, demonstrated in 1971 that this does not have to be the case. For anyone who believes in the potential of student voting as a determinative force in local politics, Iowa in 1971 provided important lessons on how to do it.

The Youth Vote in Contemporary America

Many State Laws Make It Difficult for College Students to Vote

Adam Doster

Adam Doster is a senior editor at In These Times *and a reporter-blogger for* Progress Illinois. *In the following article he describes efforts that have been made to prevent students from voting in their college towns and explains how activists are fighting back. To vote from their college address students must establish residency, but state and local election regulations on residency are not consistent and in some places have been designed to make student registration difficult. Some counties are not equipped to handle large number of registration applications, and sometimes not enough voting machines are provided in college precincts, resulting in long waits to vote. Students have challenged the legality of election board decisions under the Equal Protection Clause of the Constitution and have won some such cases. Now an organization called Student Association for Voter Empowerment (SAVE) is trying to make legislators aware of the problem and to register more young voters. Its best chance of success may lie in working with other activists who advocate election reforms.*

When the [Hillary] Clinton camp voiced displeasure with Sen. Barack Obama for encouraging Iowa-registered, out-of-state college students to participate in the Jan. 3 caucuses, her campaign was taking a student voter disenfranchisement page right out of the Republican playbook.

Take this case in Maine. In January [2007], a Republican state representative introduced LD 203, a bill that would have made Maine students ineligible to vote in their college town if they lived in university-owned housing while attending school. Proponents argued that college students, who may leave after graduation never to return, shouldn't be offered the chance to shape local policies. They also cited allegations of students casting absentee ballots in other states while simultaneously voting in Maine elections.

However, according to the secretary of state and the registrar of voters in Orono, home of Maine's flagship public university, no such voter fraud has ever been recorded. Even the bill's author confessed that he had no evidence to substantiate the accusations.

LD 203 was not the first assault on student voting rights in Maine. During the 2000 campaign, the town registrar of Brunswick, home of Bowdoin College, turned students away from the polls through deceptive residency questions. In 2002, during a close congressional contest, Henry Beck, a junior at Colby College and the youngest serving member of the Waterville, Maine, city council, says Republican operatives flooded campuses with flyers threatening that students would lose financial aid or health care if they voted at school.

But this year [2007], Maine students fought back. Activists filled hearing rooms, condemned the bill in newspaper and radio outlets, and organized online, arguing they live, work, volunteer, and pay sales taxes in their college towns. Their efforts eventually paid off, every major area newspaper denounced LD 203, and the State Senate voted it down in June.

Despite the success in Maine, student voter disenfranchisement is still prevalent across the country. As Renee Paradis, counsel for the Brennan Center for Justice at the NYU [New York University] School of Law notes, "it's been a perennial issue ever since the voting age changed." But with the 2008 election quickly approaching, students and allies are finding innovative and sustainable ways to ensure that students can register

Ella Haddix stands beside a copy of the 26th Amendment in 2006. Haddix was the first 18-year-old in the United States to register to vote under the new amendment in 1971. AP Images.

and vote in the district they prefer, and activists hope it is one cure for low voting rates among young people.

Obstacles to Student Voting

To be sure, the obstacles student voters face can be disheartening. One is the ambiguous notion of what is home. In 1979, the U.S. Supreme Court ruled that students could vote where they attend school if they "establish residency," but the court refused to qualify what constituted residency. This left the task to state and local election board members. But the patchwork system opens the door for opportunistic partisans to utilize legal harassment and red tape to suppress a crucial voting bloc. "In our experience," says Beck, "Republican operatives close to election time bring up the issue in hopes that they can complicate voting or . . . shave off a couple hundred voters in this or that college town." Officials have created residency questionnaires (much like the literacy tests of yore) specifically targeted at students, rejected registration forms from dorms, and made empty threats that students will forfeit financial aid or their child dependency status when they switch their registration information.

Identification requirements complicate the residency question. Under the 2002 Help America Vote Act, first-time voters who register by mail must present identification (a current and valid photo ID or utility bill, for example) when registering or voting. According to the Institute of Public Affairs and Civic Engagement, 11 states require multiple sources of ID to demonstrate local residency. Advocates of ID requirements say such measures are necessary to prevent fraud, and local election boards are following correct procedures when they exclude voters who don't bring the required materials. But most studies have found that ID fraud is not a serious problem, and the end result is that a student whose school and home addresses do not match is often at the mercy of local officials, many of whom are wary of the impact student voters will have on their community in the first place.

Lackluster resource allocation also negatively impacts student voting rates. For example, some counties aren't equipped to deal with a flood of registration applications just before the deadline, even though colleges are known to be hot spots for Get Out The Vote (GOTV) drives. The positioning of voting machines poses another problem. Adam Fogel, the Right to Vote program director at the Center for Voting and Democracy, was at the University of Maryland for the 2006 midterms. He noticed that a precinct catering to professors and community members was outfitted with 12 machines and had no lines all day. Meanwhile, the precinct based at the student union only housed four machines, causing four-hour backups. And while the intentionality of such placement is difficult to verify, the sheer quantity of occurrences sets off red flags. "That's not unique to Maryland," Fogel says. "It's happened at college precincts across the country, and it's an inequity."

Students denied the right to register or vote on campus can always submit a provisional ballot, but there's no assurance that those votes will be counted. According to a 2006 briefing paper by the think tank Demos, over one in three of the nearly 2 million "fail-safe" provisional ballots cast in 2004 were rejected. Absentee ballots are another, more popular option for students, but requiring voters to plan ahead can depress turnout. Voting absentee is not the most reliable method either, as half a million ballots were rejected in 2004 on (sometimes dubious) technical grounds.

The difficulty in combating misinformation is amplified because the majority of students are only affected once or twice while on the same campus. "Because students cycle out every four years," says Paradis, "it's hard to build lasting institutional memory of how you can actually guarantee everybody who wants to vote and is entitled to vote gets to vote." Many colleges and universities aren't intervening either. A 2004 study by the Harvard Institute of Politics found that 33 percent of America's colleges and universities—and 44 percent of private institutions—are not in compliance with 1998 amendments to the Higher Education Act that requires schools receiving federal funding to provide students with a mail-in voter registration form.

Students Working for Reform

Since the 2000 election, students on various campuses have contested the legality of local election board decisions, generally arguing that the Equal Protection Clause prohibits states from subjecting young people to more demanding registration requirements than other citizens. They've even won multiple cases. But thus far, the activist's approach—register as many voters as possible and litigate on a case by case basis—has been defensive and limited. So students and their allies are beginning to think strategically about ways to create lasting reforms that aren't susceptible to partisan hackery.

One such organization is the student-run, non-partisan Student Association for Voter Empowerment (SAVE), created by Matthew Segal. The Kenyon College senior became interested in voting rights [in 2004], when a lack of voting machines in Ohio forced him and some of his classmates to wait more than 10 hours to vote. "On one side, [students waiting] is a patriotic story," says Segal. "But the very fact that students had to wait in line that long showed the broken nature of our electoral system."

Prompted by that experience, Segal realized that preventing disenfranchisement required organized registration drives as well as direct lobbying for election reforms that would improve voting access. SAVE, and its 19 local chapters in Ohio, Virginia, Mississippi, and New York, has been busy at work on both fronts. A panel of students testified about barriers to registration and voting in the House Judiciary Committee hearing room in July, and local activists were encouraged to contact their state and federal representatives about the abuses. SAVE members are also working to register young people for 2008 through what they call an "institutional invasion," meaning they coordinate GOTV campaigns through institutions near their school—religious communities, public service agencies, schools—with which students are already involved. This strategy is more sustainable, they argue, because SAVE promotes strong civic education to quell misinformation and promote the value of the vote, unlike more mainstream, pop-culture infused registration drives. Elsewhere, students at New York University are teaming up with the Brennan Center to produce a state-by-state guide that will lay out the legal requirements for student voting, helping young registrants navigate the confusing and dissimilar laws.

While these are valuable first steps, young people's best opportunity to mitigate disenfranchisement may be aligning themselves with other election reform advocates. Various activists are endorsing reforms that would knock down barriers students encounter, such as establishing nonpartisan election administrations, national voting standards, and universal registration for all 18-year olds.

As Beck, Segal, and their allies know, ensuring the vote is an arduous fight. But it's one they feel is worth fighting. "It's not like voting irregularities are on the forefront of many people's minds," says Segal. "But I think these are extremely important and serious issues that are worthy of our attention and activism."

Students Can Vote in Their College Towns If They Meet Residency Requirements

Greg Abbott

Greg Abbott is the attorney general of Texas. The following view-point is an excerpt from his official opinion regarding residency requirements for college students voting in an election in the state of Texas. In it, he explains that students must meet the same residency requirements for voting as other citizens and cannot be subject to any special restrictions. This was not always the case in Texas, but a court decision struck down its former law requiring students to vote in the community where their parents reside. Furthermore, the ruling in United States v. Texas, *which was summarily affirmed by the Supreme Court in* Symm v. United States, *specifically banned the use of a residence ques-tionnaire required only of students and not of other applicants. Because of the Supreme Court ruling, this decision applies not only to Texas but to the residency requirements of other states also.*

In order to register to vote, one must be a "resident" of the county in which one desires to vote. Residence for purposes both of registration and voting is defined to mean "domicile," *i.e.*, "one's home and fixed place of habitation to which one intends to return after any temporary absence." Residence must be determined in accordance with the common-law rules, as enunciated by the courts of this state, unless the code provides otherwise. A person does not lose residence by leav-ing his home to go to another place for temporary purposes only; nor does a person acquire a residence in a place to

Greg Abbott, Attorney General's Opinion re Residency Requirement for Voting in an Election in Texas, February 4, 2004. www.oag.state.tx.us/opinions/opinions/50abbott/op/2004/pdf/ga0141.pdf.

which he has come for temporary purposes only and without the intention of making that place his home.

In the leading Texas Supreme Court case of *Mills v. Bartlett*, the court declared that the meaning of the term "residence" for voting purposes

> depends upon the circumstances surrounding the person involved and largely depends upon the present intention of the individual. Volition, intention and action are all elements to be considered in determining where a person resides and such elements are equally pertinent in denoting the permanent residence or domicile. . . . Neither bodily presence alone nor intention alone will suffice to create the residence, but when the two coincide at that moment the residence is fixed and determined. There is no specific length of time for the bodily presence to continue.

Students Cannot Be Treated Differently

Prior to *Whatley v. Clark*, students in Texas were presumed by statute to have a domicile at the residence of their parents, not where they were enrolled at institutions of higher education. *Whatley* struck down the statutory presumption in former article 5.08(k) of the Election Code providing that "'a student in a school, college, or university' shall not be considered to have acquired a voting residence at the place where he lives while attending school 'unless he intends to remain there and to make that place his home indefinitely after he ceases to be a student.'" The court noted that the statutory presumption illegally treated student voters differently than non-student voters:

> By its terms it creates a presumption that students are not domiciliaries of the places they live while attending school. Of course, the presumption is rebuttable; but unless a student carries the burden of persuading the voter registrar that he is in fact a domiciliary of the place where he resides for the better part of each year, he is not permitted to vote

there and is consequently denied an opportunity to participate in elections which may have considerably more impact
on his life than do those in the area where he resided before
becoming a student. Other prospective voters, on the other
hand, are not subject to this presumption of nonresidency
or to the attendant burden of overcoming it.

The court declared that the presumption violated the Equal
Protection Clause of the 14th Amendment and struck down
the provision.

Under current law, the determination regarding "residence"
thus involves both physical presence and current intention of
the applicant; if a student, like any other applicant, satisfies
the requirements of section 1.015, that student is a "resident"
of the county in which he seeks to register. The intention of
the voter registration applicant is crucial to a proper determination of residence, and every person is strongly presumed to
have "the right and privilege of fixing his residence according
to his own desires" *McBeth v. Streib*. For example, let us assume that two students, Student A and Student B, live in the
same college dormitory. Student A, who is living in the dormitory and is therefore physically present for purposes of
voter registration yet intends his residence to remain the same
as that of his parents, can permissibly register to vote in the
county of his parent's residence. *See, e.g., Alvarez v. Espinoza*
(by temporarily moving to Austin to attend school at the University of Texas at Austin, challenged voter did not lose his
Frio County residence or acquire residence for voting purposes in Travis County). On the other hand, Student B, who is
living in the same dormitory as Student A yet who intends
that the dormitory be his residence for purposes of voter registration, can permissibly register to vote in the county where
his dormitory is located. *See, e.g., Whatley* (student who was
physically present in Denton County and intended to claim
Denton County as his residence for purposes of voter registration lost residence in the county where his parents resided

and acquired residence in Denton County). And the mere fact that an applicant claims a post office box as an address or that many applicants claim the same post office box as an address is not dispositive regarding the determination of residence. Indeed, depending upon the facts in each case, it might not even be relevant. *See, e.g., Speights v. Willis* (voters who were physically present and intended county to be residence for purposes of voter registration, yet who claimed post office box numbers as addresses, satisfied statutory voter registration application requirements and, thereby, residence requirement).

The Supreme Court Ruling

Without outlining all of the various fact situations that the courts have addressed in determining whether a voter is a "resident," we can say that all applicants for registration, including students, must be subject equally to whatever presumptions or restrictions are imposed by law. To illustrate the sorts of factors and practices that cannot be employed to determine "residence," we examine the federal three-judge panel's injunction in *United States v. Texas*, affirmed [by the Supreme Court in] *Symm v. United States* (1979) (hereinafter *Texas*). ... Though in a brief submitted to this office the Criminal District Attorney of Waller County seems to assert that the case only prohibited the use of a certain questionnaire in determining "residence" for purposes of voter registration, the injunction issued in the case makes it clear beyond cavil [trivial objection] that the court concluded that a variety of practices undertaken by the voter registrar violated the United States Constitution.

In *Texas*, a federal three-judge panel enjoined the Waller County Tax Assessor-Collector, who was the voter registrar, from refusing to register to vote students enrolled at Prairie View A&M University. Specifically, the panel enjoined the registrar from engaging in a variety of practices that the panel deemed violated the 26th Amendment to the United States

Constitution, which provides that no right of citizens who are 18 years old or older to vote shall be denied or abridged on account of age.

The panel ordered that, *inter alia* [among other things], college students of Waller County must be registered and allowed to vote on the same basis and by application of the same standards and procedures as non-students, without reference to whether such students had dormitory addresses, whether or not they resided in Waller County prior to attending school, and whether or not they planned to leave Waller County upon graduation. The panel acknowledged that the registrar had the authority under the Election Code to make a factual determination as to whether each applicant to vote was a bona fide [genuine or authentic] resident of Waller County; however, in making this factual determination, the panel declared that the registrar could not find that a person was a non-resident of Waller County for any of the following reasons:

1. That such person resides in a dormitory at Prairie View A&M University;
2. That such person owns no property in Waller County;
3. That such person is a student at Prairie View University;
4. That such applicant has no employment or promise of employment in Waller County;
5. That such applicant previously lived outside Waller County, or may live outside Waller County after his graduation;
6. That such person visits the home of his parents, or some other place during holidays and school vacations.

The panel required that, if the registrar made a finding that a person was not a bona fide resident of Waller County, the determination must be made on the basis of tangible evidence, consisting of facts or factors other than the six factors listed above. In addition, in the event that the registrar made a determination that any person who claims to be a resident of Waller County, and who had a Prairie View A&M University address, was not a bona fide resident of Waller County, the registrar must make a written record of the precise, exact tangible evidence upon which he relied in making his determination of non-residency. . . .

Additionally, students of Waller County were not to be subjected to the presumption contained in former article 5.08(k) of the Election Code or to any other presumption with regard to their voting residence. The registrar was ordered immediately to cease using the residence standard for students, which had been implemented by means of a questionnaire, to terminate the use of the questionnaire, and to henceforth register students on the basis of the information contained in the state-approved registration form, as was done elsewhere in Texas, unless the registrar had tangible, recordable evidence that such applicant was not a bona fide resident of Waller County. And the registrar was enjoined from subjecting Prairie View A&M students to any particular or discriminatory procedure not applied to non-students on a regular basis, such as, for example, causing students to visit his office and submitting students orally to the questioning previously contained in the questionnaire discussed in the court's Memorandum Opinion.

We stress that the United States Supreme Court affirmed the three-judge panel's judgment in *Symm v. United States*, clearly, in light of *Whatley* and *Texas*, students in Texas may no longer be subjected, whether by statute or by practice, to any presumption with respect to "residence" not also applied to all other voters in Texas.

The Right of Students to Vote in Their College Towns Is Often Misinterpreted

Michael I. Krauss

Michael I. Krauss is a professor of law at George Mason University. In the following viewpoint he points out that prior to the 2008 election Barack Obama's Web site sometimes gave advice to students about registering to vote that was not always legal and that encouraged actions that might be harmful to them in the future. It advised students whose college addresses were in "battleground" states to register at those addresses, not their parents' addresses. However, Krauss contends, while it is often said that the Supreme Court has ruled that students have a right to vote at their college addresses, that is a misinterpretation of the ruling. The Court held merely that students must be treated like everyone else seeking to register and cannot be subject to restrictions not applicable to nonstudents. They must meet the same standards of residency as all others, and this requires an honest belief that a voter intends to reside indefinitely in the area where he or she votes. Furthermore, students need to consider all the potential consequences of changing their legal residence, which may affect such things as taxes, insurance coverage, and residence-dependent scholarships. Krauss maintains that registering to vote is a fundamental right of citizenship that should not be undertaken dishonestly.

Are you a college student seeking to register to vote? Barack Obama's website makes it easy. But does the site follow the law? Let's take a look.

First the site asks, "Where will you be living on Election Day, November 4th?" Next it asks, "Is there another state

Michael I. Krauss, "The Obama College Try," *National Review Online*, October 2, 2008. Reproduced by permission. http://article.nationalreview.com/?q=MWRjYjllZTgx
ZTk3Zjg5NjkyYmRmYzU3YTJjOTk3NDg.

where you might be registered?" Presumably, many college students who attend school in one state but live with their parents in another will answer this question in the affirmative. The answers to these two questions prompt curious suggestions from the Obama website.

If the respondent states that she is registered to vote at her parents' home in Pennsylvania (a "battleground" state) but will be in her dorm in New York (a safe Obama state) on Election Day, the website recommends that the student vote by absentee ballot in Pennsylvania. No problem there—that is the legal solution in most cases. But if the respondent says she is registered in New York but studying in battleground Pennsylvania, Obama recommends that she register to vote in Pennsylvania (and presumably de-register in New York)!

Clearly, Obama is trying to switch voter registration of Democrats (who are, of course, more likely to go to his website than are Republicans) to battleground states such as Virginia, where I work. This campaign tactic raises legal and ethical questions. Is Sen. Obama's campaign encouraging voter fraud? Is it encouraging college students to take actions that may be harmful without informing them of relevant risks? If so, what does this say about the integrity of the campaign?

Ruling Often Misinterpreted

First, the law. A September 8 [2008] *New York Times* article headlined "Voter Registration by Students Raises Cloud of Consequences" states that a Supreme Court case has held that "students have the right to register at their college address." That's at best an incomplete, and at worst a misleading, statement of the law. The article refers to *Symm v. United States*, a 1979 case affirming (without discussion) a decision by a special three-judge district-court panel.

That panel had held that LeRoy Symm, a county commissioner, had erred when determining whether a young college student could vote in his district. The case reiterates not that college students have an automatic right to vote where they are studying, but merely that they must be treated like anyone else who applies to register to vote in the county. In other words, states and counties may ask reasonable questions about legal residency and the eligibility to vote of college students, and they may require documentary support for the student's claims, but only if they apply the same rules to all would-be voters.

Relying perhaps on the same inaccurate interpretation of *Symm*, the ACLU of Virginia faxed a letter to Virginia voting registrars on September 4, insisting that students have the right to register where they go to school. According to the ACLU, Virginia registrars must register students if they "have a local residential address," without "any special inquiries or burdens."

Again, this is misleading; students may register where they attend college only if they meet the same standards of residency applicable to all others applying to vote. These standards may include signing affidavits or showing residence-based identification (such as a driver's license), even if the ACLU considers that to be a "special" inquiry. By a curious coincidence, five days after the ACLU letter was faxed, the Virginia State Board of Elections published guidelines that allow students to claim residence in Virginia unchallenged. Courageously, the City of Norfolk Office of Elections (which consists of two Democrats and one Republican) has declared that though it will abide by this executive-branch directive, it firmly believes the directive violates Virginia election laws.

All this is enough to make one wonder whether a move is afoot in battleground states governed by Democratic administrations to allow vote-shifting from other states. But that is not all—in addition to legal problems, the Obama campaign's enticement of student re-registration is ethically suspect. Changing one's legal residence requires a student's honest belief that she intends to reside indefinitely at her new residence, the college town. Sometimes this is doubtful (do Washington and Lee students really intend to reside indefinitely in tiny Lexington, Va.?).

Legal Consequences

A less-than-truthful declaration could catch up with the declarant in future years, if he or she contemplates a career requiring vetting or close press scrutiny. But even if an honest student has suddenly acquired the intention of residing indefinitely in his college town, does he understand the legal implications of a residence change? Where is the student filing her income-tax return (will she be liable for another state's tax)? Is the student claimed as a dependent on her parents' return (if so, it is hard to have a separate legal residence)? Does the student have a residence-dependent scholarship (some require that recipients reside in a particular town or state) that might be imperiled by a change of residence? Would the student's automobile or health-insurance coverage be affected by a change in residence, especially if the student is covered by her parents' policy? Apparently the Obama campaign feels no compunction against warning students that disingenuous declarations of residency may have consequences in the future.

Registering to vote is a fundamental rite of citizenship. It is not to be undertaken frivolously and dishonestly. Shame on anyone who manipulates this process in order to tamper with our electoral-college system of state-based presidential elections.

Students Are Sometimes Given Inaccurate Information About Voter Registration

Elizabeth Redden

Elizabeth Redden is a reporter for Inside Higher Ed, *an online news site. In the following article she discusses a press release on student voter registration issued by Montgomery County, Virginia, that some observers felt was designed to discourage students from voting in their college communities. The people interviewed for the article said many of the warnings it contained, which were also being given to students in other states, were far-fetched and misleading. It is untrue, they said, that students will lose their tax status as dependents of their parents if they do not reside at the same address, because there is an exemption in the U.S. tax law allowing dependents to live away from home while attending school. The county registrar maintained, however, that while the county does not want to suppress student voting, students need to investigate the possible consequences of changing their residence and that the political campaigns objecting to this are concerned only with getting more voters signed up.*

Last week [September 2008] Virginia's Montgomery County, home to Virginia Tech, issued a press release regarding proper protocol for college students registering to vote. In interviews with *Inside Higher Ed*, it was described by turns as "unsubstantiated," "chilling," and (more generously) as not "incredibly encouraging or friendly."

It reads, in part: "The Code of Virginia states that a student must declare a legal residence in order to register. A legal residence can be either a student's permanent address from home or their current college residence. By making Montgomery County your permanent residence, you have declared your independence from your parents and can no longer be claimed as a dependent on their income tax filings—check with your tax professional. If you have a scholarship attached to your former residence, you could lose this funding. And, if you change your registration to Montgomery County, Virginia Code requires you to change your driver's license and car registration to your present address within 30 days."

The county registrar of elections said that the memo was intended to counteract the absence of cautionary information given to students signed up through the ubiquitous get-out-the-vote registration drives. Generally speaking, however, those interviewed for this article said the warnings are, at worst, far-fetched and misleading, or, at best, overstated and not typically supported in reality.

And, in a year in which historic youth voter turnout is anticipated, and the Democratic presidential candidate, Barack Obama, has been propelled by college students' support, this case in the battleground state of Virginia is "not an isolated incident," said Sujatha Jahagirdar, program director for the Student Public Interest Research Group's nonpartisan New Voters Project.

Unsubstantiated Warnings

"For a county registrar to issue what really are in our experience unsubstantiated warnings for a particular demographic is alarming," said Jahagirdar. "It's upsetting that this is coming up in Virginia. But it's even more upsetting that the ability of young people to vote is questioned in many other states too."

She added: "In 25 years of registering young voters around the country, none of the staff has ever heard of a single incident where a student has lost their tax status or their scholarship because of where they've registered to vote."

Meanwhile, Obama's campaign, which has been registering voters on Virginia Tech's campus, has called the information propagated by the county "erroneous." The campaign's Virginia spokesman, Kevin Griffis, cited an exemption in the U.S. tax code allowing dependents to live away from home while attending school.

And he said that while students should check with their individual health insurers, in the campaign's calls to 10 top health insurance companies, none indicated that registering to vote at a college address would be grounds for dismissing students from coverage, "and in fact some of them laughed at us." (In an interview with *Inside Higher Ed*, Lynne High, a spokeswoman for the mammoth United Healthcare, echoed that students covered on their parents' health insurance plans aren't affected if they register to vote in another state.)

"We should be trying to engage as many people as possible in the political process, and have them take part in the civic life of their communities. In the case of students at Virginia Tech, their community is Blacksburg. That's where they live; that's where they call home. They should be able to vote there," Griffis said. (The campaign of the Republican presidential nominee, John McCain, did not return a call to its Virginia state office Tuesday.)

Montgomery County followed up its first dispatch with a somewhat more neutrally worded news release two days later, on August 27. This one raised similar issues but in the form of questions, which students were prompted to consider in deciding whether to register to vote where their family lives or where their college is.

Among them: "Are you claimed as a dependent on your parents' income tax return? If you are, then their address is probably your legal residence. . . . Do you have a scholarship that would be affected if you changed your legal residence?. . . Would your health, automobile or other insurance coverage be affected by a change in your legal residence? If you are covered under your parents' insurance policy, your protection could be affected by a change in your legal residence."

The language in the county's second release was taken from the Virginia State Board of Elections' Web site, which in itself is discouraging, said Jon Greenbaum, director of the Voting Rights Project at the Lawyers' Committee for Civil Rights Under Law, in Washington. "If you were to look at this as a student, the suggestion that the State Board of Elections is giving you is, 'You probably should not register to vote here. Don't register to vote here.' We think that's the wrong message to be sending."

Lack of Information

In an interview, E. Randall Wertz, the general registrar of elections for Montgomery County, cited the State Board of Election's guidance on college student registration as what he relied upon. He explained that, in sending the memo, he was attempting to combat either the misinformation, or lack of information, that college students have to consider when signing up through voter registration drives.

"What's happening is they're going out across campus over here and just getting people to sign the registration forms left and right and not telling them issues to consider, or telling them the incorrect information," said Wertz. "Before they make the decision to register with us, they need to check with the accountant who does the taxes. They need to check if they're on their parents' health insurance. By being at a separate permanent address, does that affect their insurance?"

"I was just trying to inform them of things to consider, and then once they've made an informed decision and decide to come with us, we welcome them," Wertz said.

"We don't want to suppress them from voting and we certainly want them to vote. It's just, what's best for them is what they need to consider. Unfortunately, the campaigns, they're not concerned with what's best for the student. They're gener-ally concerned with just getting people signed up."

Voter registration drives at Virginia Tech brought more than 2,000 new registrations to the county, Wertz said. He also estimated that about 25 students have called to ask if the county could cancel the processing of their registration.

The Twenty-sixth Amendment Should Be Repealed

Timothy Furnish

Timothy Furnish is an assistant professor of history at Georgia Perimeter College in Atlanta. In the following viewpoint he argues that giving eighteen-year-olds the vote was a mistake. It is not true, he says, that democracy works best when the franchise is extended to as many Americans as possible. It is best when knowledgeable *citizens vote, and he feels that teenagers are not knowledgeable—as a history professor he has found that they are ignorant of basic facts about history and government. While there is no guarantee that voters over thirty are better informed than those just out of high school, it is likely that they are, because they have had experience in college, the business world, or the military. In Furnish's opinion it would be a good idea to require young people to earn the right to vote by serving two years either in the military or as civil volunteers. At the very least, he says, there should be some sort of test to demonstrate that their ignorance of public affairs is not total. In his opinion the Twenty-sixth Amendment should be repealed.*

President [Richard] Nixon is usually denigrated for Watergate, his "enemies list," even his participation in post–World War II anti-Communist fervor. But there was a blunder committed by the 37th president that far outstrips all his others combined. That was signing the 26th Amendment into law in 1971, giving 18-year-olds the right to vote.

Lowering the voting age such that all college freshmen, and even many high school seniors, could help choose the Republic's leaders was undoubtedly one of the dumbest things

Timothy Furnish, "Should We Take Away the Voting Rights of 18 Year Olds?" *History News Network*, November 15, 2004. Reproduced by permission. http://hnn.us/articles/8491.html.

ever done in this country's history. We can't totally blame Nixon, since this misguided movement had been supported earlier by President [Dwight] Eisenhower and [Lyndon] Johnson and, of course, practically the entire Congress in Nixon's time. May they all fry in one of [Italian poet] Dante's lowest circles of Hell for this transgression against political sense.

What is wrong with such young folks voting? Doesn't democracy work better when the franchise is extended to as many Americans as feasibly possible? And isn't it true that "old enough to die, old enough to vote?"—as the amendment's supporters argued during the Vietnam War?

To answer these questions in reverse order: no, no and *Are you kidding?!*. Democracy works when *knowledgeable* citizens vote, as was recognized as long ago as Plato's and Aristotle's time. Can any rational member of the human species watch [comedian] Jay Leno's "Jaywalking"—in which he roams the streets of Southern California, interviewing folks who don't know the vice president's name, which hemisphere they live in—and possibly think it's a good idea for these people to be left alone with a voting machine of any kind?

Too Ignorant to Vote

As a college history professor, I can cite examples of 18- and 19-year olds' ignorance that make the Jaywalkers look like the Founding Fathers. One of my students recently announced that he'd received a *draft notice* in the mail (can anyone say "Stripes?"). No one in an entire modern world history class this term knew when the American Revolution began. When I queried my classes "what is the approximate size of the U.S. budget for the upcoming fiscal year?" most replies ranged between a few hundred million dollars and a few billion (the actual figure is about $2 and 1/2 trillion). Most of my students thought that the African-American population made up "30 or 40 percent" of the U.S., whereas it's actually 12.5 percent.

Actor Rosario Dawson makes an appearance on MTV at the MTV studios in New York in 2004. Dawson helped organize a campaign aimed at drawing youth and minority voters to the polls. AP Images.

Many of my students have written, on tests or papers, that Jesus is worshipped by the Jewish people and that Muhammad lived before Jesus. (Shouldn't voters know something about the world's major religions?) And I have had many students who thought that Nazi Germany used nuclear weapons in World War II (in which case wouldn't we all be goose-stepping and speaking Deutsche?).

My point is not to score cheap points at my students' expense. (Almost all of them, after all, went to public school in Georgia—the state that ranks 49th in SAT scores—and most of us college professors here have resigned ourselves to the fate of repairing the damage done by secondary school teachers—which might be worth contemplating the next time public school teachers are demanding yet another pay raise.) The point is that we allow such uninformed people to vote! Indeed, we encourage it: MTV's "Rock the Vote," [entertainer] P. Diddy's "Vote or Die." There's even an organization, "Youthrights.org," that demands we lower the voting age to 16! (Just what we need: presidential candidates taking stands on their preferred anti-acne medication.)

Now there is no guarantee that a 30-something voter will be more informed than one just out of high school—but it's a good bet. As Michael Barone points out in his book *Hard America, Soft America*, this nation's 18-year olds are, on average, coddled, spoiled and ignorant; but by the time they hit their third decade, most of them are extremely competent and productive (thanks to good colleges, the business world or the military).

Right to Vote Should Be Earned

So I won't go as far as my wife, who cites Barone to advocate 30 as the minimum voting age. I'll settle for raising it to 20— with a major caveat, addressing the "old enough to die, old enough to vote" argument. The late science-fiction writer Robert Heinlein, in his book *Starship Troopers* (try to pretend you've never seen the horrible movie, [actress] Denise Richards notwithstanding), posited a futuristic world government which worked extremely well because of one thing: only those who had proved their dedication to the collective good, by volunteering for the military, could vote. So let's set up a similar system, with both a military and civil volunteer component (in the latter those opposed to warfare could help with international disaster relief, for example), requiring a two-year minimum stint. Thus one could join right out of high school, at 18, and then when the term of service was up at 20 the right to vote would follow. Two years in such an environment would not only demonstrate the individual's seriousness about citizenship, it would almost undoubtedly educate them beyond the level of the modern Jaywalker or college undergrad.

If that smacks too much of social engineering, let's at least institute a qualifying quiz for voters, of perhaps three questions: 1) what's the square root of 16? 2) who is your current congressional representative? 3) what part of the U.S. is now being referred to as "Jesusland?" Or devise your own questions—but we need some litmus test that demonstrates the prospective voter knows *something* and has not just been demagogued into believing that the GOP [Republican Party] wishes to starve senior citizens or that the Democrats want [terrorist Osama] Bin Ladin to move into the Oval Office.

We dodged a bullet in [the 2004] election, when the ignorant youth masses turned out in record numbers (51 percent of the 18–29 year olds voted; figures for [the] subslice of that pie that includes only 18–20 years olds is unavailable), which broke for [John] Kerry by about 10 points. Only the fact that most other age groups voted in even larger numbers drowned out the callow masses' otherwise influential cluelessness. One would like to think that even Democrats "win at any price" desperation stops just short of encouraging Know Nothings to support them. So I say: dock their vote! Repeal the 26th Amendment before President P. Diddy is sworn in.

The Voting Age Should Be Lowered to Sixteen

National Youth Rights Association

The National Youth Rights Association (NYRA) is a youth-led national nonprofit organization dedicated to fighting for the civil rights and liberties of young people. In the following statement from its Web site, it presents what it believes to be the top ten reasons for lowering the voting age to sixteen. Teens have adult responsibilities without adult rights, NYRA says. They pay taxes and live under the same laws as adults. If sixteen-year-olds could vote, politicians would have a reason to represent their interests. NYRA argues that it would be better to introduce voting to young people while they are settled in communities than when they have just moved away for college or work. The earlier in life the habit of voting is formed, the more likely they will be to go on voting when they are older. And since ignorant and incompetent adults are allowed to vote, there is no reason to withhold the vote from teens on the basis of their being uninformed. Schools may establish classes to prepare young voters. And finally, granting them the right to vote would increase young people's sense of responsibility and push them to become involved, active citizens.

"No right is more precious in a free country than that of having a choice in the election of those who make the laws under which ... we must live. Other rights, even the most basic, are illusory if the right to vote is undermined."
—*Wesberry v. Saunders, 1964*

National Youth Rights Association, "Top Ten Reasons to Lower the Voting Age," National Youth Rights Association, September 25, 2008. Reproduced by permission. www.youthrights.org/vote10.php.

Top Ten Reasons to Lower the Voting Age:

Youth Suffer under a Double Standard

In 1971 the United States ratified the 26th Amendment to the Constitution granting the right to vote to 18–20-year-olds. The 26th Amendment was the fastest to be ratified in U.S. history. At the height of the Vietnam War most Americans realized the sick double standard inherent in sending 18-year-old soldiers to fight and die for their country when they weren't allowed to vote. Double standards didn't go away in 1971. Right now youth are subject to adult criminal penalties despite lacking the right to vote.

[Historian] Frank Zimring found that "Between 1992 and 1995, forty American states relaxed the requirements for transferring an accused under the maximum age of jurisdiction into criminal court," and "In Colorado, for example, defendants under the maximum age for juvenile court jurisdiction may nonetheless be charged by direct filing in criminal court if they are over 14 years of age and are charged with one of a legislative list of violent crimes."

What kind of twisted message do we send when we tell youth they are judged mature, responsible adults when they commit murder, but silly, brainless kids when they want to vote? This is a double standard, no different than during the Vietnam War. War isn't a dead issue now either, leaders who youth can't vote for today may send them to war tomorrow. Lowering the voting age is the just, fair way to set things straight.

Youth Pay Taxes

Just like all other Americans, young Americans pay taxes. In fact, they pay a lot of taxes. Teens pay an estimated $9.7 billion in sales taxes alone. Not to mention many millions of taxes on income. According to the IRS, "You may be a teen, you may not even have a permanent job, but you have to pay taxes on the money you earn." And teens do work: 80% of high school students work at some point before graduation. Youth pay billions in taxes to state, local, and federal governments yet they have absolutely no say over how much is taken. This is what the American Revolution was fought over; this is taxation without representation.

In addition to being affected by taxes, young people are affected by every other law that Americans live under. As fellow citizens in this society, every action or inaction taken by lawmakers affects youth directly, yet they have no say in the matter. In her 1991 testimony before a Minnesota House subcommittee, 14-year-old Rebecca Tilsen had this to say:

"If 16-year-olds are old enough to drink the water polluted by the industries that you regulate, if 16-year-olds are old enough to breathe the air ruined by garbage burners that government built, if 16-year-olds are old enough to walk on the streets made unsafe by terrible drugs and crime policies, if 16-year-olds are old enough to live in poverty in the richest country in the world, if 16-year-olds are old enough to get sick in a country with the worst public health-care programs in the world, and if 16-year-olds are old enough to attend school districts that you underfund, then 16-year-olds are old enough to play a part in making them better."

The just power of government comes from the consent of the governed. As it stands now youth are governed (overly so, some may say) but do not consent. This is un-American. Like all tax-paying, law-abiding Americans, youth must be given the right to vote.

Politicians Will Represent Their Interests If Youth Can Vote

Politicians represent various constituencies; currently young people are no one's constituency. Why should politicians care about the needs and wishes of youth when they have no ability to vote for or against them? Lowering the voting age will give politicians a real reason to respect the desires of young people.

Youth feel alienated from politics and politicians, lowering the voting age will include them in the process. The words spoken before the Senate Judiciary Committee supporting lowering the voting age in 1971 are as true then as they are now: "The anachronistic voting-age limitation tends to alienate them from systematic political processes and to drive them to into a search for an alternative, sometimes violent, means to express their frustrations over the gap between the nation's deals and actions. Lowering the voting age will provide them with a direct, constructive and democratic channel for making their views felt and for giving them a responsible stake in the future of the nation."

Youth Have a Unique Perspective

A common argument against lowering the voting age is that it isn't a burden to wait a few years. Denying youth the right to vote isn't the same as denying women or racial minorities, according to opponents, since in a few years young people will grow up and be able to vote. Why go through the trouble to lower the age to 16 when after two years they'll be able to vote anyways? Were it that simple, then perhaps, but it isn't.

Would it be acceptable to limit the right to vote to those with a certain income, reasoning that it is a flexible standard, those with less income must only work harder or wait till they too make enough to vote? No it wouldn't. Voters vote based on their individual circumstances, when those circumstances change often so do their voting habits. The concerns of a 14 year old are different than that of a 24 year old, just as the concerns of a poor man differ from that of a rich man. The beliefs and priorities of 16 year olds as a class are unique to them; we cannot expect former 16 year olds to have as accurate a perspective as those who are currently that age. If we care at all about the needs and desires of youth, they must be allowed to vote for themselves.

What Teens Think About Lowering the Voting Age to 16 or 17

	13–14 yr-olds	15–17 yr-olds	Female	Male
Question 1: Do you think you are responsible enough to (check all that apply)				
Drive a car	81.9%	94.6%	90.9%	89.0%
Vote	69.9%	79.6%	79.7%	71.4%
Speak at a town hall meeting	43.5%	50.7%	49.1%	37.0%
Enlist in the army	29.8%	37.8%	20.3%	42.9%
Run for office	28.8%	22.8%	19.8%	21.1%
Question 2: . . .when would you give people the right to vote?				
Age 16	49.7%	28.2%	24.1%	40.9%
Age 17	12.6%	19.7%	21.3%	21.7%
Age 18	26.2%	40.5%	43.7%	29.4%
Age 19–21	11.6%	11.6%	10.9%	7.9%
Question 3: In your opinion, what percentage of 16 year-olds are qualified to vote?				
0	18.3%	11.6%	14.1%	20.2%
1/4	33.0%	49.6%	48.7%	38.5%
1/2	21.5%	22.8%	25.4%	22.1%
3/4	18.8%	13.3%	8.5%	8.8%
All	8.4%	2.7%	3.2%	10.5%
Question 4: In your opinion, what percentage of 17 year-olds are qualified to vote?				
0	16.2%	6.5%	8.3%	13.3%
1/4	20.4%	28.9%	25.1%	18.4%
1/2	27.2%	30.3%	33.0%	30.9%
3/4	22.5%	27.2%	26.4%	24.1%
All	19.6%	22.5%	7.2%	13.4%

[CONTINUED]

[CONTINUED]

What Teens Think About Lowering the Voting Age to 16 or 17

	13–14 yr-olds	15–17 yr-olds	Female	Male
Question 5: Would you sign a petition lowering the voting age to 17?				
Yes	58.6%	51.0%	54.7%	72.5%
No	20.4%	30.3%	45.3%	27.5%
Don't Know	20.9%	18.7%	n/a	n/a

TAKEN FROM: Do Something, Inc.

---

16 Is a Better Age to Introduce Voting than 18

Currently the right to vote is granted at perhaps the worst possible moment in one's life. At 18 many youth leave the home and community they have lived [in] for most [of] their life, either to go away to college or to move away from home in search of work. At the moment they are supposed to vote they either have a new community that they are unfamiliar with or they must attempt to vote absentee back home, a process that turns off many new voters.

Lowering the voting age to 16 will give the vote to people who have roots in a community, have an appreciation for local issues, and will be more concerned about voting than those just two years older. Youth have comfortable surroundings, school, parents, and stable friends, they feel connected to their community; all factors that will increase their desire and need to vote. Lower the voting age, and youth will vote.

Lowering the Voting Age Will Increase Voter Turnout

For several reasons lowering the voting age will increase voter turnout. It is common knowledge that the earlier in life a habit is formed the more likely that habit or interest will continue throughout life. If attempts are made to prevent young people from picking up bad habits, why are no attempts made to get youth started with good habits, like voting? If citizens begin voting earlier, and get into the habit of doing so earlier, they are more likely to stick with it through life.

Not only will turnout increase for the remainder of young voter's lives, the turnout of their parents will increase as well: A 1996 survey by Bruce Merrill, an Arizona State University journalism professor, found a strong increase in turnout. Merrill compared turnout of registered voters in five cities with Kids Voting with turnout in five cities without the program. Merrill found that between five and ten percent of respondents reported Kids Voting was a factor in their decision to vote. This indicated that 600,000 adults nationwide were encouraged to vote by the program.

Kids Voting is a program in which children participate in a mock vote and accompany their parents to the polls on Election Day. Reports show that even this modest gesture to including youth increased the interest in voting of their whole family. Parents were more likely to discuss politics with their kids and thus an estimated 600,000 adult voters were more likely to vote because of it. Lowering the voting age will strengthen this democracy for all of us.

If We Let Stupid Adults Vote, Why Not Let Smart Youth Vote?

The argument that youth "should not vote because they lack the ability to make informed and intelligent decisions is valid only if that standard is applied to all citizens" [writes Richard Farson in his book *Birthrights*]. But yet this standard is not applied to all citizens, only young people. "We do not deprive a senile person of this right, nor do we deprive any of the millions of alcoholics, neurotics, psychotics and assorted fanatics who live outside hospitals of it. We seldom ever prevent those who are hospitalized for mental illness from voting."

Even beyond senile, neurotic, and psychotic adults, regular adults often do not meet the unrealistic standard opponents to youth voting propose. Turn on the Tonight Show one night and see the collection of adult buffoons who can't tell Jay Leno who the vice-president is, or who have forgotten how many states are in this country. Yet these adults are happily given the right to vote. The fact is, intelligence or maturity is not the basis upon which the right to vote is granted, if that were the case all voters would need to pass a test before voting. Though "... under voting rights jurisprudence, literacy tests are highly suspect (and indeed are banned under federal law), and lack of education or information about election issues is not a basis for withholding the franchise," [writes Samuel Davis, in *Children in the Legal System.*] Youth shouldn't be held to a stricter standard than adults; lower the voting age.

Furthermore, even the federal government agrees that most youth have the necessary knowledge to vote. The Voting Rights Act of 1965 states that: "any person who has not been adjudged an incompetent and who has completed the sixth grade in [...] any State or territory, the District of Columbia, or the Commonwealth of Puerto Rico where instruction is carried on predominantly in the English language, possesses sufficient literacy, comprehension, and intelligence to vote in any election." If a sixth grade education is deemed adequate knowledge to vote, how can older youth be denied the right to vote?

Youth Will Vote Well

It is silly to fear that huge masses of youth will rush to the voting booth and unwittingly vote for Mickey Mouse and Britney Spears. By and large, those individuals with no interest in politics and no knowledge on the subject will stay home from the polls and not vote. This mechanism works for adult voters as well. Youth will behave no differently.

Besides foolishly throwing a vote away, some worry about youth voting for dangerous radicals. These fears are unfounded as well. [As John Holt writes in *Escape from Childhood,*] "We should remember, too, that many people today vote at first, and often for many years after, exactly as their parents voted. We are all deeply influenced, in politics as everything else, by the words and example of people we love and trust." [Young people's] political leanings are influenced by their community and their family, and it is likely young voters will vote in much the same way as their parents, not because they are coerced to do so, but because of shared values.

With the voting age at 16 there is the opportunity for new voters to have a greater opportunity to be educated voters as most are in high school. When the voting age is lowered schools will most likely schedule a civics class to coincide with 16 that will introduce the issues and prepare new voters. It stands to reason that these young voters will be better prepared to vote than their elders.

There Are No Wrong Votes

Noting that youth will most likely vote well we must wonder, is it at all possible for a voter to vote wrong? Did voters choose poorly when they elected [Bill] Clinton in 1996? Republicans would say so. Did voters choose poorly when they elected [George W.] Bush in 2004? Democrats would say so. If youth were able to vote for either of them, or against them, would they be voting wrong? [National Youth Rights Association doesn't] think so. All voters have their own reasons for voting, we may disagree with their reasons, but we must respect their right to make a decision. This is what we must do with youth.

Lowering the Voting Age Will Provide an Intrinsic Benefit to the Lives of Youth

Granting youth the right to vote will have a direct effect on their character, intelligence and sense of responsibility. Is it any wonder why many youth feel apathetic towards politics? After 18 years of their life being told their opinion doesn't matter, they are just foolish children who should be seen and not heard, is anyone surprised that many people over 18 feel turned off by politics and don't vote? We can see this contrast between volunteering and politics. Teenagers have amazingly high levels of volunteering and community service, however many feel turned off by politics. Even small gestures like mock voting has a large effect on teens' interest in politics, of students participating in Kids Voting USA. More than 71% of students reported frequently or occasionally questioning parents about elections at home. These same students also viewed voting with great importance. About 94% felt it was very important or somewhat important to vote. Including youth in a real, substantive way in politics will lead to even more interest as they take their public-spirited nature into the political realm.

Many opponents [of] lowering the voting age assume apathetic youth today will be no different when given the right to vote; this is wrong. Responsibility comes with rights, not the other way around. "It is not a pre-condition of self-government that those that govern be wise, educated, mature, responsible and so on, but instead these are the results which self-government is designed to produce," [writes Avrum Stroll in the *Journal of Value Inquiry*.] Educator and youth rights theorist John Holt points out that if youth "think their choices and decisions make a differences to them, in their own lives, they will have every reason to try to choose and decide more wisely. But if what they think makes no difference, why bother to think?" He stresses this point again, "It is not just power, but impotence, that corrupts people. It gives them the mind and soul of slaves. It makes them indifferent, lazy, cynical, irresponsible, and, above all, stupid."

Lowering the voting age may not be the magic bullet to improve the lives of youth, but by giving them a real stake in their futures and their present lives it will push them to become involved, active citizens of this great nation. The National Youth Rights Association strongly urges lawmakers and individuals in this country to seriously consider lowering the voting age.

Sixteen-Year-Olds Should Become Politically Active to Gain the Vote

Ralph Nader

Ralph Nader is a well-known author and political activist who has run several times as an independent candidate for president of the United States. In the following viewpoint he argues that sixteen-year-olds are likely to be more excited about voting than eighteen-year-olds who are away from home and must obtain absentee ballots, and that their interest would encourage their parents to vote. Also, he says, high school teachers would offer more nonpartisan information about candidates if their students could vote. Austria has already lowered its voting age to sixteen, and several other countries, as well as several U.S. states, are considering doing so. However, Nader says, in order to gain the vote teens must become active and recognize the responsibilities of citizenship. They can spread ideas faster than any generation in history because of Web sites such as YouTube, MySpace, and Facebook. But they should not rely entirely on the Internet because rallies, marches, and group visits to legislators are also needed. Nader favors the sixteen-year-old vote, but in his opinion it will not become a reality unless a teenage political revolution makes it happen.

You are sixteen. You can legally work, drive a motor vehicle and with parental consent get married in most states. Why can't you legally vote?

Good question, and one that supporters for dropping the voting age from eighteen to sixteen will be asking politicians more and more. Much has been made of the youth vote this

Ralph Nader, "Disenfranchised Youth," *Counterpunch*, June 4, 2008. Reproduced by permission of the author. www.counterpunch.org/nader06042008.html.

year [2008] amid evidence that more young people are turning out to vote in the primaries than ever before. Let's take it to the next step.

I argued for the voting age drop from twenty one to eighteen back in the Sixties before it finally happened in 1971 with the ratification of the Twenty-Sixth Amendment to our Constitution. The absence of a vibrant civic culture inside and outside our schools drained away much of the potential of this electoral liberation for youngsters. Their turnout was lower than older adults.

Sixteen-year-olds are likely to be more excited. They are studying and learning about the country and the world in high school. They're still at home and can bring their discussions to their parents, who may turnout at the polls more as a result.

Fifteen-year-old Danielle Charette, writing last January [2008] in the *Hartford Courant*, says: "Consumed in the distraction of their first semester at college, many eligible voters fail to arrange for absentee ballots. Of course, if annual voting became more habitual starting in high school, reading up on the candidates and voting while away from home wouldn't seem out of the ordinary."

Moreover, social studies teachers in high school would be keener on non-partisan class analyses of candidates if their students were able to vote.

Ms. Charette made another telling point. Sixteen-year-olds who also work pay taxes but they have no vote. This is "taxation without representation," she exclaimed.

International Examples

Austria lowered its voting age to 16 last year [2007], prompting similar proposals by New Zealand legislators. One Swiss Canton [political district] (Glarus) lowered the voting age to participate in local and cantonal elections to 16 in 2007. Brit-

Ralph Nader, an author and political activist who has been running as a presidential candidate in elections since 1996, gives a speech at press conference. In 1971, Nader argued for the voting age to be lowered from twenty-one to eighteen, and he now advocates the age to be lowered to sixteen. AP Images.

ish member of Parliament, Sarah McCarthy-Fry expects a debate on the 16- year-old vote issue soon in the House of Commons.

Austrian Social Democrat Chancellor Alfred Gusenbauer said that lowering the voting age was a "challenge to Austria's school system" in the field of political education. While New Zealand MP [member of Parliament] Sue Bradford ties this voting reform in her proposed legislation with making civics education compulsory in high school to enhance students' understanding of the political system.

Some States Have Considered Lowering the Voting Age

Bills in Minnesota and Michigan have been introduced to lower the voting age. Their rationale is to give a "real opportunity for young people to vote on something that affects their daily lives," according to Sen. Sandy Pappas of St. Paul.

Now it's time to hear from these young Americans. They can exchange and spread words faster and cheaper than any generation in history—what with YouTube, MySpace and Facebook communications.

Here is some advice to them: First don't just make it a matter of your voting right as "citizens now," not citizens in waiting. Recognize your responsibilities and duties of engaged citizenship.

Second, raise some compelling changes and redirections that will improve life in America especially for you and generally for all Americans. You know lots of them. Just ask yourself, as you shop, study, work, play, breathe the air and drink the water, and watch the TV news, what kind of country do you want to see in the coming months and years?

To jumpstart the 16-year-old voting movement, youngsters need to start jumping. Needed are rallies, marches, and personal group visits to your members of Congress and state legislatures at their local offices, especially when the lawmakers are not in session and are back in their home communities.

Don't over rely on the Internet. The impact from showing up in person is far greater.

I'll be talking up the sixteen-year-old vote. But it will only become a reality if a teenage political revolution makes it happen.

Appendices

Appendix A

The Amendments to the U.S. Constitution

Amendment I: Freedom of Religion, Speech, Press, Petition, and
                   Assembly (ratified 1791)
Amendment II: Right to Bear Arms (ratified 1791)
Amendment III: Quartering of Soldiers (ratified 1791)
Amendment IV: Freedom from Unfair Search and Seizures
                   (ratified 1791)
Amendment V: Right to Due Process (ratified 1791)
Amendment VI: Rights of the Accused (ratified 1791)
Amendment VII: Right to Trial by Jury (ratified 1791)
Amendment VIII: Freedom from Cruel and Unusual Punishment
                   (ratified 1791)
Amendment IX: Construction of the Constitution (ratified 1791)
Amendment X: Powers of the States and People (ratified 1791)
Amendment XI: Judicial Limits (ratified 1795)
Amendment XII: Presidential Election Process (ratified 1804)
Amendment XIII: Abolishing Slavery (ratified 1865)
Amendment XIV: Equal Protection, Due Process, Citizenship for All
                   (ratified 1868)

The Amendments to the U.S. Constitution

Amendment XV: Race and the Right to Vote (ratified 1870)
Amendment XVI: Allowing Federal Income Tax (ratified 1913)
Amendment XVII: Establishing Election to the U.S. Senate
(ratified 1913)
Amendment XVIII: Prohibition (ratified 1919)
Amendment XIX: Granting Women the Right to Vote (ratified 1920)
Amendment XX: Establishing Term Commencement for Congress
and the President (ratified 1933)
Amendment XXI: Repeal of Prohibition (ratified 1933)
Amendment XXII: Establishing Term Limits for U.S. President
(ratified 1951)
Amendment XXIII: Allowing Washington, D.C., Representation in the
Electoral College (ratified 1961)
Amendment XXIV: Prohibition of the Poll Tax (ratified 1964)
Amendment XXV: Presidential Disability and Succession
(ratified 1967)
Amendment XXVI: Lowering the Voting Age (ratified 1971)
Amendment XXVII: Limiting Congressional Pay Increases
(ratified 1992)

Appendix B

Court Cases Relevant to the Twenty-sixth Amendment

Whittingham v. Board of Education, 1970
A New York court upheld a state law requiring student voter registration applicants to prove their residence by some indication other than enrollment at a local college.

Anderson v. Brown, 1971
An Ohio court ruled that a law that mandated different residency requirements for students from those of all other voting-aged people was in violation of the equal protection clause.

Bright v. Baesler, 1971
A Kentucky court ruled that the alleged discrimination against young voters was based on student status, not age, and so the case must be decided on equal protection grounds rather than on the basis of the Twenty-sixth Amendment. (Other courts have cited this precedent.)

Harris v. Samuels, 1971
The Fifth Circuit Court decided that the federal courts should not intervene with respect to an Alabama state law under which some students had not been allowed to vote at their college address before the state courts had interpreted that law.

Jolicoeur v. Mihaly, 1971
A California court ruled that a law creating a presumption that an unmarried student's residence was his or her parents' home violated the Fourteenth and Twenty-sixth Amendments, stating that "a youth will not be brought into the bosom of

the political system by being told that he may not vote in the community in which he lives, but must vote wherever his parents live or may move to."

Shivelhood v. Davis, 1971
A Vermont court ruled that the government may not require that student applicants for voting registration answer different questions than those asked of nonstudent applicants.

Wilkins v. Bentley, 1971
A Michigan court ruled that for the state to presume that students were not voting residents unless they proved it through procedures applying only to students violated their right of equal protection under the law.

Gorenberg v. Onondaga County Board of Elections, 1972
A New York court upheld a state law specifying criteria for determining residence that included dependency, employment, marital status, age, and location of property.

Palla v. Suffolk County Board of Elections, 1972
A New York court ruled that to be a resident of a place, a person must be physically present with the intent to remain for a time.

Ramey v. Rockefeller, 1972
A New York court ruled that the only constitutionally permissible test for voting residence "is one which focuses on the individual's present intention and does not require him [or her] to pledge allegiance for an indefinite future."

Reed v. City of Cambridge, 1972
The First Circuit Court declined, for technical reasons, to decide whether the refusal to register certain students was unconstitutional and stated that the election board should have "an opportunity to evolve procedures to meet the needs created by the adoption of the Twenty-sixth Amendment."

Sloane v. Smith, 1972
A Pennsylvania court prohibited election officials from applying voter registration standards to students different from those applied to nonstudents.

Worden v. Mercer County Board of Elections, 1972
A New Jersey court stated that the purpose of the Twenty-sixth Amendment was not only to extend the voting right to younger voters but also to "encourage their participation by the elimination of all unnecessary burdens and barriers."

Walgren v. Howes, 1973
The First Circuit Court ruled that the district court should not have dismissed a case concerning a local election held during winter break when students—about 30 percent of the town's population—were away, and remanded it for further consideration. In so ruling, it stated, "The specific problem faced by college communities with concentrated youth populations was faced in the consideration of the Twenty-Sixth Amendment. To the expressed fears of campus takeovers of small communities . . . the candid response in debate was that if students 'satisfy the residency requirement of that town obviously they would be entitled to vote.'"

Whatley v. Clark, 1973
The Fifth Circuit Court ruled that a Texas law stating that students are not eligible to vote at their college residences unless they intend to remain permanently in the community was unconstitutional under the Equal Protection Clause because, although the same standard was required of other voters, the law created a presumption that students were transient and required them to prove otherwise.

Ballas v. Symm, 1974
The Fifth Circuit Court held that the use of a questionnaire to determine eligibility to vote was not unconstitutional discrimination, since it applied not just to students but also to other people not personally known to the registrar.

Dyer v. Huff, 1974

The Fourth Circuit Court affirmed a South Carolina court's opinion that a board of elections "would be derelict in its duty to blindly accept a statement of residency by each applicant. There is nothing wrong or even suspect in registration officials asking college boarding students, whose permanent addresses are outside the county, certain questions to determine residency."

Hershkoff v. Worcester, 1974

A Massachusetts court ruled that support by parents or dormitory residence cannot be used to limit a young voter's freedom of choice of domicile.

National Movement for the Student Vote v. University of California, 1975

A California court ruled that a university regulation prohibiting canvassing by voter registrars in dormitory living areas was a reasonable protection of students' privacy, even though local law permitted registering voters at their place of residence.

Walgren v. Amherst, 1975

In a follow-up to *Walgren v. Howes*, the First Circuit Court held that for a local election to be held during winter break when most students are away is permissible, since not all of them leave and those who do can vote by absentee ballot. The court declined to rule on the issue of whether such scheduling violates the Twenty-sixth Amendment, nevertheless stating, "It is difficult to believe that it contributes no added protection to that already offered by the Fourteenth Amendment, particularly if a significant burden were found to have been intentionally imposed . . . on the exercise of the franchise by the benefactors of that amendment."

Cesar v. Onondaga County Board of Elections, 1976

The New York Supreme Court ruled that while the requirements for establishing residency for voting purposes are an intent to reside at a fixed place and a personal presence at that place, the facts supporting such an intent must be wholly independent of the applicant being a student and that "present intention" does not "require him to pledge allegiance for an indefinite future."

United States v. Texas, 1978
A federal court prohibited a Texas county registrar from requiring student applicants for voter registration to complete a questionnaire that was not required of other applicants, ruling that this violated the Twenty-sixth Amendment. (In 1979 this decision was summarily affirmed by the U.S. Supreme Court in *Symm v. United States.*)

Lloyd v. Babb, 1979
A North Carolina court held that "a student who intends to remain in his college community only until graduation should not for that reason alone be denied the right to vote in that community."

Auerbach v. Kinley, 1980
A New York court ruled that merely being a student is not a basis for being denied voter registration.

DuBois v. City of College Park, 1980
A Maryland court ruled that a reapportionment plan for city council districts that excluded a large segment of students who lived in university dormitories violated the Equal Protection Clause of the Fourteenth Amendment.

Harrell v. Southern Illinois University, 1983
An Illinois court ruled that a university regulation prohibiting political canvassing in dormitory rooms except during designated hours was not an infringement of free speech.

Wray v. Monroe County Board of Elections, 1984
A New York court, citing *Auerbach v. Kinley*, held that the state "has a right to ascertain whether applicants for registration to vote are bona fide residents, but that it must do so in a way that does not violate the applicant's constitutional right to be treated on an equal basis with other citizens."

Auerbach v. Rettaliata, 1985
The Second Circuit Court ruled that for a state to identify classes of likely transients and make inquiries about their residence before registering them to vote does not violate the Equal Protection Clause, but that students cannot be singled out for stricter scrutiny than other classes.

Williams v. Salerno, 1986
The Second Circuit Court ruled that a state cannot have a per se rule against registering voters who reside in student dormitories because "although students living in dormitories may often lack the intent to remain in the place where they attend school, it is certainly possible for a person to abandon his or her former residence with the intent to remain in the place where he or she attends school."

Levy v. Scranton, 1991
A New York court held that college students had been unconstitutionally denied the right to vote solely because they lived in on-campus housing.

Scolaro v. District of Columbia Board of Elections and Ethics, 1997
The District of Columbia Circuit Court ruled that community residents may not challenge the registration of student voters merely on a presumption that they reside elsewhere and that the board has no duty to scrutinize students applicants who have signed forms stating that they are eligible to register.

Regensburger v. City of Bowling Green, 2002
The Sixth Circuit Court ruled that the city's reapportionment violated the rights of students because the ward in which the campus was located had more than twice as many residents as other wards, thus diluting their votes.

U.S. Student Association Foundation v. Land, 2008
The Sixth Circuit Court denied Michigan's appeal for a stay against an injunction to prevent it from rejecting a voter's reg-

istration when that voter's identification card was returned to election officials as undeliverable.

For Further Research

Books

Bower Aly, ed., *Youth Suffrage*. Columbia, MO: Lucas Brothers, 1944.

David E. Campbell, *Why We Vote: How Schools and Communities Shape Our Civic Life*. Princeton, NJ: Princeton University Press, 2006.

Michael Connery, *Youth to Power: How Today's Young Voters Are Building Tomorrow's Progressive Majority*. Brooklyn: Ig, 2008.

Wendell W. Cultice, *Youth's Battle for the Ballot: A History of Voting Age in America*. New York: Greenwood, 1992.

Russell J. Dalton, *The Good Citizen: How a Younger Generation Is Reshaping American Politics*. Washington, DC: CQ Press, 2008.

Robert E. DiClerico, *Voting in America: A Reference Handbook*. Santa Barbara, CA: ABC-CLIO, 2004.

Declare Yourself, *Speak, Connect, Act, Vote: More than 50 Celebrated Americans Tell You Why*. New York: Greenwillow Books, 2008.

Frederick G. Dutton, *Changing Sources of Power: American Politics in the 1970's*. New York: McGraw-Hill, 1971.

Jane Eisner, *Taking Back the Vote: Getting American Youth Involved in Our Democracy*. Boston: Beacon, 2004.

Lorn S. Foster, ed., *The Voting Rights Act: Consequences and Implications*. New York: Praeger, 1985.

Benjamin Griffith, *America Votes! A Guide to Modern Election Law and Voting Rights*. Chicago: American Bar Association, 2008.

David Hill, *American Voter Turnout: An Institutional Perspective.* Boulder, CO: Westview, 2006.

Alexander Keyssar, *The Right to Vote: The Contested History of Democracy in the United States.* New York: Basic Books, 2000.

Garrine P. Laney, *The Voting Rights Act of 1965 as Amended: Its History and Current Issues.* New York: Nova Science, 2008.

Brian D. Loader, ed., *Young Citizens in the Digital Age: Political Engagement, Young People, and New Media.* New York: Routledge, 2007.

Kevin Mattson, *Engaging Youth: Combating the Apathy of Young Americans Toward Politics.* New York: Century Foundation Press, 2003.

Spencer Overton, *Stealing Democracy: The New Politics of Voter Suppression.* New York: Norton, 2006.

Frances Fox Piven and Richard A. Cloward, *Why Americans Still Don't Vote: And Why Politicians Want It That Way.* Boston: Beacon, 2000.

Rick Shenkman, *Just How Stupid Are We? Facing the Truth About the American Voter.* New York: Basic Books, 2008.

Donald Grier Stephenson, *The Right to Vote: Rights and Liberties Under the Law.* Santa Barbara, CA: ABC-CLIO, 2004.

Ruy A. Teixeira, *The Disappearing American Voter.* Washington, DC: Brookings Institution Press, 1992.

———, *Why Americans Don't Vote: Turnout Decline in the United States, 1960–1984.* Westport, CT: Greenwood, 1987.

Martin P. Wattenberg, *Is Voting for Young People?* New York: Pearson/Longman, 2007.

————, *Where Have All the Voters Gone?* Cambridge, MA: Harvard University Press, 2002.

Raymond E. Wolfinger and Steven J. Rosenstone, *Who Votes?* New Haven, CT: Yale University Press, 1980.

Periodicals

Kathleen Barr and Tom Evans, "Is This Really the Year of the Youth Vote?" *Politics*, October 2008.

Pam Belluck and Patricia Smith, "16 Candles and a Ballot?" *New York Times Upfront*, January 14, 2008.

Richard L. Berke, "Is the Vote, Too, Wasted on Youth?" *New York Times*, June 30, 1991.

Damien Cave, "Mock the Vote," *Rolling Stone*, May 27, 2004.

K. Crawford, "Youth Is Served: Senate Votes to Lower Voting Age," *Newsweek*, March 30, 1970.

Cora Currier, "Generation O," *Nation*, March 3, 2008.

Tim Dickinson, "The Youth Vote," *Rolling Stone*, November 11, 2004.

Janet Elder, "Courting the Youth Vote," *New York Times Upfront*, September 3, 2007.

Julie Flaherty, "Voting Rights for 17-Year-Olds," *New York Times*, March 27, 2002.

Fred P. Graham, "New Law on Voting Rights at Age 18 Is Denounced Before Supreme Court by Lawyers for Four States," *New York Times*, October 20, 1970.

Kendra Hamilton, "The Power of the Youth Bloc," *Black Issues in Higher Education*, October 7, 2004.

Anya Kamenetz, "You're 16, You're Beautiful and You're a Voter," *New York Times*, February 6, 2008.

Nathan Levin, "Bizarre Discussion by the Court: The Sometime 18-Year-Old Vote," *New Republic*, January 2, 1971.

Tamar Lewin, "Voter Registration by Students Raises Cloud of Consequences," *New York Times*, September 7, 2008.

Adam Liptak, "1971: 18-Year-Olds Get the Vote," *New York Times Upfront*, September 4, 2006.

Shawn Macomber, "Suffer the (Political) Children," *American Spectator*, October 2008.

John Allan May, "Youth Vote Could Reshape Politics and Elections," *Christian Science Monitor*, April 14, 1970.

Newsweek, "Age of Aquarius: Senate Amendment to Enfranchise Eighteen-Year-Olds," March 23, 1970.

Michael Novak, "Let a Million Voters Bloom," *Commonweal*, April 12, 1971.

Tim O'Brian, "The Youth Vote," *New Republic*, August 19, 1972.

Alan L. Otten, "Hello Young Voters," *Wall Street Journal*, January 7, 1971.

Ari Pinkus, "Young Voters Beat a Path Toward a Politics Of Morals," *Christian Science Monitor*, April 12, 2006.

Bret Schulte, "A Push for the Youth Vote," *U.S. News & World Report*, October 22, 2007.

Nikki Schwab, "Teach Your Children How to Vote," *U.S. News & World Report*, December 31, 2007.

Richard E. Singer, "Home Is Where the Vote Is," *Nation*, September 13, 1971.

David Skaggs and Adam Anthony, "Winning with Young Voters," *Campaigns & Elections*, August 2002.

David Von Drehle et al., "It's Their Turn Now," *Time*, February 11, 2008.

Tully E. Warren, "The Youth Vote: What Is Its Importance?" *Vital Issues*, no. 9, 1973.

Mattie Weiss, "Mobilize the Millennials," *Campaigns & Elections*, December 2007.

Theodore H. White, "The Theology of the Youth Vote," *New York Times*, January 6, 1971.

John K. Wilson, "The Attack on Student Voting Rights," *Inside Higher Ed*, December 31, 2007.

Internet Sources

Melissa Dahl, "Youth Vote May Have Been Key in Obama's Win," *MSNBC.com*, November 5, 2008. www.msnbc.msn.com.

E.J. Dionne, "The Year the Youth Vote Arrives," *Real Clear Politics*, July 25, 2008. www.realclearpolitics.com.

Max Fisher, "Silencing the Students," *New Republic* (Web only), October 9, 2008. www.tnr.com.

David Paul Kuhn, "Obama Has Historic Youth Mandate," *Politico*, November 11, 2008. www.politico.com.

Amanda Ruggeri, "Young Voters Powered Obama's Victory While Shrugging Off Slacker Image," *U.S. News & World Report* (Web only), November 6, 2008. www.usnews.com.

Nikki Schwab, "Confusing Voter Registration Laws Could Affect Presidential Election," *U.S. News & World Report* (Web only), September 24, 2008. www.usnews.com.

David Von Drehle, "The Year of the Youth Vote," *Time* (Web only), January 31, 2008. www.time.com.

Geoff Ziezulewicz, "Overseas Voting Is Not Just a Duty, It's a Chore," *Stars and Stripes*, August 24, 2008. www.stripes.com.

Web Sites

CIRCLE: Center for Information and Research on Civic Learning and Engagement, www.civicyouth.org. A nationally known organization that conducts research on the civic and political engagement of Americans between the ages of fifteen and twenty-five. It offers statistics and fact sheets on the youth vote as well as other topics related to citizenship.

Mobilize.org, www.mobilize.org. An all-partisan network dedicated to educating, empowering, and energizing young people to increase civic engagement and political participation

NYRA: National Youth Rights Association, www.youthrights.org. A national youth-led organization that defends the civil and human rights of young people in the United States through educating people about youth rights, working with public officials, and empowering young people to work on their own behalf. It advocates allowing younger teens to vote.

Rock the Vote, www.rockthevote.com. Rock the Vote's mission is to engage and build the political power of young people in order to achieve progressive change in America. It uses music, popular culture, and new technologies to engage and incite young people to register and to vote in every election.

SAVE: Student Association for Voter Empowerment, www.savevoting.org. A national nonprofit organization founded and run by students. It aims to increase youth voter turnout by removing access barriers and promoting stronger civic education.

Youth Vote Overseas, https://yvo.overseasvotefoundation.org. A nonpartisan organization that provides information and online voter registration tools to U.S. citizens overseas, including service members.

Index